GET REAL!

A NEW WINDMILL BOOK OF NON-FICTION

**EDITED BY
DAVID KITCHEN AND SUE DAVIES**

Heinemann
New Windmills

Heinemann Educational Publishers
Halley Court, Jordan Hill, Oxford OX2 8EJ
A division of Reed Educational and Professional Publishing Ltd

OXFORD MELBOURNE AUCKLAND
JOHANNESBURG BLANTYRE GABORONE
IBADAN PORTSMOUTH (NH) USA CHICAGO

03 02 01 00 99
10 9 8 7 6 5 4 3

ISBN 0 435 13042 0

Acknowledgements

The Editors and Publishers would like to thank the following for permission to use
copyright material:

Scholastic Ltd. for extracts from 'Time to sleep it off' from *Seriously Weird True Stories* by Herbie
Brennan, text copyright © Herbie Brennan 1997, page 1; from 'The Stomach for the Job' from *Blood,
Bones and Body Bits* by Nick Arnold, text copyright © Nick Arnold 1996, page 5; and from 'A Little
Stabbing' from *The Terrible Tudors* by Terry Deary and Neil Tonge, text copyright © Terry Deary and
Neil Tonge 1993, page 99. Macmillan Publishers for an extract from *Mukiwa: A White Boy in Africa* by
Peter Godwin, 1996, page 15. David Higham Associates on behalf of Sue Sharpe for an extract from
Voices From Home, Virago, 1990, page 21. Bloomsbury Publishing Plc, for an extract from *I Must Tell
You Something* by Arno Bo, 1996, page 39. Penguin Books Ltd for an extract from *Zlata's Diary* (pp.38–
46) by Zlata Filipovie, translated by Christina Pribichevich-Zoric (Viking 1994, first published as *Le
Journal de Zlata* by Fixot et editions Robert Laffont, 1993), copyright © Fixot et editions Robert Laffont,
1993, page 48; for an extract from *The UFO Investigator's Handbook* (pp.18–29) by Marc Gascoigne
(Puffin 1996), copyright © Marc Gascoigne 1996, page 83; and for an extract from *Tell No One Who You
Are* (pp.24–25, 30–33) by Walter Buchnignani (Puffin 1997), copyright © Walter Buchnignani 1994.
Fourth Estate Ltd. for an extract from *The Diving Bell and the Butterfly* by Jean-Dominique Bauby,
translated by Jeremy Leggatt, copyright © Editions Robert Laffont, S.A. 1997. Translation copyright ©
Editions Robert Laffont, S.A. 1997, page 56. Reader's Digest Ltd for an extract from *The Amazing World
of Nature* by Ronald N. Rood, copyright © 1969, page 76. HarperCollins Publishers for an extract from
Arthur C. Clark's Amazing World of Mysteries edited by Simon Welfare and Brian Fairley, page 74, and
for an extract from *The Young Person's Guide to UFOs* by Brian Ball, 1979, page 86. Rowan Wilson for an
extract from *UFOs – Strange but True* (Robinson Publishing) and for an extract from *World
Famous Robberies*, page 104 (Magpie Books). Nigel Blundell for extracts from *Daring Vagabonds and
Villains*, page 109. Transworld Publishers Ltd. for an extract from *The Lost Continent* by Bill Bryson,
page 115 (Black Swan, a division of Transworld Publishers Ltd.), copyright © Bill Bryson 1989. All rights
reserved. Peter Hain for extracts from his article 'When Coal was King' published *The Sunday Times* 23
August, 1989, page 120. John Murray (Publishers) Ltd. for an extract from *The Spirit of St. Louis* by
Charles Lindbergh, page 124. Honno, Welsh Women's Press for an extract from 'Bombs and
Beachcombing' by Dorothy Thomas in *Parachutes and Petticoats* edited by Leigh Verrill-Rhys and
Deidre Beddoe, page 135. Walker Books Ltd., London, for an extract from *Ordinary Seaman* by John
Gordon, copyright © John Gordon 1992, page 140. Anita Naik for an extract from *Coping with Crushes*
(Sheldon Press 1994), page 151. Piccadilly Press Ltd. for an extract from *Staying Cool Surviving School*
by Rosie Rushton, copyright © 1993, page 157. Oxford University Press for an extract from *The Diary of
a Teenage Health Freak* by Aidan Macfarlane and Ann McPherson, 1987, page 161.

The Publishers have made every effort to trace the copyright holders, but if they have inadvertently
overlooked any, they will be pleased to make the necessary arrangements at
the first opportunity.

Cover design by The Point
Cover illustration by Aldo Balding
Typeset by Tek-Art, Croydon, Surrey
Printed and bound in the United Kingdom by Clays Ltd, St Ives plc

Contents

Introduction for teachers

In putting together this collection of non-fiction, our priority has been to find material that is interesting and engaging but that also allows students to become familiar with a wide range of non-fiction material. For this reason, we spent a lot of time trying the passages out in our own schools before we arrived at a final draft.

By the end of Key Stage 3, students should have come into contact with a wide range of non-fiction, including autobiography, biography, diaries, articles and letters. They should be able to select information relevant to their purpose, make effective use of information in their own work and evaluate how information is presented. We have therefore devised a number of activities which offer opportunities to practise all of these skills, both in order to meet the requirements of the National Curriculum and to provide students with skills they will need in later life.

Although research has shown that non-fiction material is of particular interest to boys, we have found that the material chosen appeals to a large number of pupils, both boys and girls. We hope, therefore, that you find this collection effective as a resource that stimulates and motivates all your Key Stage 3 students.

Introduction for students

If you ask any group of young people about fiction, they are clear about what the word means and who likes to read what. Ask that same group about non-fiction and the answers can vary enormously.

Some will tell you that non-fiction is simply books full of facts. Well, there are plenty of facts here but there are also opinions and ideas.

Others will tell you that non-fiction does not contain any stories. Not true. There are as many stories here as you are likely to find in most novels. The difference is that they are stories about people's lives.

Who reads non-fiction? Many people will tell you that non-fiction is basically for boys rather than girls. If you look at the pattern of book buying, that would seem to be at least partly true. On the other hand, take a look at the selection here and you will find something for everyone.

If you do not normally read non-fiction, we hope this book will encourage you to look a little more closely at what there is on offer. If you already like this kind of writing, we hope that you will be stimulated to explore further what is available.

Section 1
Phenomenon

People have always had a special interest in things that cannot easily be explained. Even when something can be understood, it may often seem strange or unusual. This section looks at three matters that fit under the 'strange but true' banner. It starts with the longest sleep on record.

Time to sleep it off
Herbie Brennan

When you are not feeling one hundred per cent, your parents may tell you to go to bed and try to sleep it off. Perhaps that is what happened with Carolina Olsson. If they did say anything like that, they must have regretted it many times during the next few years. Anyway, here is her story.

Fourteen-year-old Swedish schoolgirl, Carolina Olsson, was on her way home to the family cottage at Oknö, near Mönsteras, in February, 1876, when she slipped on the ice and fell, hitting her head.

By the time she got home, she had a nasty headache and a couple of days later started to complain about tiredness. Her mother put her to bed.

On the evening of 22 February, 1876, Carolina fell asleep. She slept soundly until 3 April, 1908.

For the first couple of days and nights, Carolina's parents debated about calling the doctor. Her father was a fisherman, far from rich, and wasn't sure he could afford the fee. They fed her milk and sugared water and hoped she would eventually wake up.

When she didn't, they finally called a doctor. He examined her, stuck needles into her fingers to test for a reaction, then pronounced his diagnosis. The girl, he said, was in a deep sleep.

This was the first of many unhelpful medical opinions. Word of Carolina's condition went the rounds and more and more doctors took an interest. Many had their own ideas about her condition. They said she was supposed to be suffering from paralysis or faking.

But no one had any idea how to wake her up.

In desperation, her parents brought her to Oskarhamn Hospital where the doctors tried to wake her by giving her electric shocks. When that didn't work, they sent her home. Her condition, they said, was incurable.

One night her father came in from work to discover Carolina kneeling by the sofa where she slept, praying to Jesus. He was overjoyed until he realized she was not awake, but sleepwalking. When she finished her prayers, she climbed back into bed.

The family kept feeding her milk and sugared water. Carolina kept sleeping. When her mother died in 1908, a widowed neighbour came in to help with the housekeeping.

On 3 April, 1908, thirty-two years and forty-two days after she dozed off, Carolina eventually awoke. The housekeeper found her wandering about the cottage looking for her mother.

It was a painful awakening. Not only was her mother gone, but two of her brothers were also dead, the result of a drowning accident. She could not believe that her father was now old and her remaining brothers middle-aged. She remembered them as they had been more than thirty years before.

Oddly enough, while her family had aged, Carolina hadn't – or at least not at anything like the same rate. Her body still looked like that of a fourteen-year-old and while her face seemed a little older, nobody would have taken her for anything older than her middle twenties, although she was in fact forty-six.

Not surprisingly, Carolina found herself famous. The newspapers dubbed her Sleeping Beauty (she was a very pretty girl) and tourists turned up by the coachload just to catch a glimpse of her.

She was a little weak and dizzy immediately after wakening, but demanded a meal of herring and quickly recovered.

Some two years after her ordeal she was examined by a doctor from Stockholm. He found her intelligent and cheerful, healthy and co-operative. She still looked far younger than her actual age and had a clear memory of her life before she fell asleep.

Her life after she woke up again proved long and happy. She survived a further forty-two years and died, aged 89, in April, 1950.

• One of the oddest aspects of Carolina Olsson's weird experience was that neither her hair, her toe-nails nor her fingernails grew while she was asleep. This is particularly bizarre when you remember that the fingernails and hair of a corpse continue to grow for some time after death.

• Although widely studied, Carolina's condition was a mystery to the medical profession and remains so today. Although she was often referred to as being in a coma, this actually seems unlikely: most coma victims die without regaining consciousness, or are disabled when they do waken. Carolina's sleep gave her no problems at all.

• Unless you follow Carolina's example, you will spend about a third of your life sleeping. This means that if you live as long as she did, you will have rested about thirty years in the Land of Nod. If this sounds surprisingly close to Carolina's own record, you have to remember she stayed asleep for thirty-two years *continuously*. Furthermore, she would *already* have spent approximately four to five of her previous fourteen years in normal sleep. When she woke after her big sleep, her normal sleep pattern would account for a further twelve years until the time of her death. So Carolina Olsson, at 89, had actually spent about fifty years sleeping during her lifetime.

The stomach for the job
Nick Arnold

'There are no such things as problems,' say some
people, 'there are only opportunities.' It is doubtful
whether Alexis St. Martin would have agreed with them
when, in 1822, a gun exploded and nearly killed him.
The strange thing is that Alexis' suffering turned into an
amazing opportunity for the doctor who was called out
to help him.

The young man moaned in agony. A carelessly loaded
shotgun had exploded – blasting a 15 cm (6 inch) hole in
Alexis St. Martin's side . . . you could see all his insides.
The young Canadian hunter had two broken ribs, a
damaged lung and . . . a hole in his stomach.

Dr William Beaumont looked at these injuries and
shook his head sadly. The patient would die soon. Very
soon. In those days the only treatment for this type of
wound was to slap on a bandage and arrange the funeral.
But against all expectations, Alexis survived the night.
Weeks became months and the young man even started
to get better! But he had an embarrassing problem.

The stomach hole refused to heal. So whenever he
felt peckish Alexis had to bandage his tum to stop its
gruesome contents from slopping out!

Oddly enough the young man cheerfully put up with
this appalling arrangement. So the devious doctor seized
the opportunity to perform some gruesome gut
experiments. One day he asked Alexis to swallow a bit of
raw meat on a thread. Later he pulled it up again to see
how it had changed. On another occasion Dr Beaumont

poked a thermometer through the hole and watched it leap about as the stomach churned!

The doctor soon discovered that stomach juice is produced in large amounts when there's food in the stomach. So he drained some of Alexis's stomach juice out through a pipe and tried to identify the chemicals it contained. First of all he tasted it – YUCK! But as he wasn't sure what it was he sent it to some scientist friends. They discovered the juice contained hydrochloric acid – a powerful dissolving chemical. This is useful for breaking down food and killing germs.

Sometimes the doctor and his patient would have a row. You've got to see it from Alexis' point of view. For two years Dr Beaumont had nursed him. But on the other hand . . . well, if there's one thing worse than having a hole in your body – it's being chased around by a meddlesome medic trying to terrorise your tummy. And over the next few years Dr Beaumont took to following Alexis so he could perform even more horrible experiments!

Oddly enough these shouting matches provided Dr Beaumont with yet more sickening scientific data. He couldn't help noticing that when Alexis got cross, his stomach went all red and quivery!

At last in 1833 Dr Beaumont published his findings. It had taken 11 years of tests and tantrums. Packed full of stomach-churning pictures, the book was an overnight success. The doctor achieved fame and fortune. Yet he owed his entire achievement to one gruesome fact . . . he'd had the stomach for the job!

Can anything travel faster than light?
Barry Zimmerman and David Zimmerman

If science from the past provides some strange stories, science in the future may provide even stranger ones. For example, the possibility of travelling not only faster than sound but faster than light . . .

> Captain James T. Kirk looked at the starboard screen in dismay. 'Warp 3, Scotty,' he said. 'The Klingons are gaining on us.'
>
> 'Aye, Captain,' the first engineer answered, boosting the engines of the USS *Enterprise* into the *faster-than-light* warp drive.

This 'Star Trek'-inspired dialogue may sound familiar to you. In science fiction, faster-than-light travel is accepted as reality. How else could it be possible for humans to journey across the galaxy to explore other stars and other worlds? Traveling *at* the speed of light, the very nearest star (aside from the Sun) is more than four years away, and most stars are *thousands* of years away. But can spaceships travel at 'warp' speeds – faster than light? Can anything travel faster than light?

To answer these questions we must first ask, How fast does light travel? This is not an easy question to answer. Light does not always travel at the same speed. Can you run as quickly on sand at a beach as you can on a track? Of course not. Light also has more difficulty traveling through some substances, or media, than it does through others. It travels slower in diamond than it does in glass, slower in glass than it does in water, slower in water than it does in air, and slower in air – though only slightly – than it does in nothing (a *vacuum*). Light, in fact, travels faster in a vacuum than it does anywhere else. But how fast is that?

A beam of light (or any other form of electromagnetic radiation, such as X rays, microwaves, or radio waves) travels at a speed of 186,291 miles/second (299,792 kilometers/second). At this speed, it would travel around the world *more than seven times* in one second! It would travel to the moon in less than two seconds and to the Sun in about eight minutes. In air, light travels nearly *one million* times faster than sound.

The speed of light was first determined with accuracy by a French physicist, Armand H. L. Fizeau, in 1849. The value was refined by a co-worker of Fizeau's, Jean B. L. Foucault, and later by Albert A. Michelson, an American physicist who devoted fifty years of his life to the search for the true speed of light. During 1923 and 1924, in California, Michelson performed a classic experiment using a powerful beam of light, mirrors, and two mountaintops 22 miles (about 35 km) apart, measuring with an error of *less than one inch*. He got a value for the speed of light that was accurate to within several thousandths of 1 percent. His work on light helped earn Michelson the Nobel Prize in physics, the first American to achieve this honor.

Let us now return to our original question: Can anything travel faster than light? Since light travels at different speeds in different media, we must restate the question, being more specific: Can anything travel faster than light *in a vacuum*? The answer is no. The speed of light in a vacuum is the limit at which anything – matter or energy – can travel. But why is that? Why can't we take a car or rocket ship and keep on accelerating it, feeding it more and more fuel, making it go faster and faster, until it reaches and surpasses the speed of light?

Take a golf ball, for instance. As it sits on the tee, its speed is zero. When the golfer whacks it with the head of the club, the energy from the moving club is transferred to the ball as energy of motion. A well-hit golf ball may easily attain a speed of 100 miles/hour (160 km/hour). This speed, however, is still about *six million* times slower than the speed of light in a vacuum. But what if the golf ball could be hit six million times harder? Would it not then travel six million times faster, or at the speed of light?

No, it would not. The reasons why this is not possible are complicated and mathematical. Strange things happen as an object approaches light speed. When energy is imparted to an object (such as a golf ball when the golf club hits it), that energy can be used in one of two ways. It can be transferred as energy, causing the object to move faster, or it can be converted into mass, causing the object to have more matter. At all normal speeds, even speeds thousands of times faster than a speeding golf ball, energy imparted to matter is transferred almost entirely as energy. In other words, if you hit a golf ball, it goes faster. As one approaches light speed, however, more and more of that energy is converted into mass, and less is transferred as energy. The object does not speed up as much as it increases its matter. *At* the speed of light, *all* the energy that one puts into an object is converted into mass. A golf ball that is traveling at the speed of light cannot speed up any more. If additional energy were put into it, that energy could not be transferred as energy of motion but would instead be converted entirely into mass. The golf ball would not go faster; it would get more massive. In fact, as one gets very close to the speed of light, so much of the energy is converted to mass that it is virtually impossible for an object to even reach the speed of light in a vacuum.

Scientists have come close, however – though not with golf balls or cars or rocket ships. Using very powerful devices called particle accelerators, scientists have gotten subatomic particles such as electrons, which are extremely small and light and easy to speed up, to travel at speeds close to 186,291 miles/sec.

Another strange thing that happens at near-light speeds has to do with time. As matter travels faster, time slows down. This slowing is not noticeable at ordinary speeds. If you are traveling in a car at 60 mph or in an airplane at 600 mph, time does not slow down enough to be noticed. Your watch would be moving at about the same rate as the watches of people not moving at all. But if you were traveling in the USS *Enterprise* with Captain Kirk at 186,000 miles per *second*, time would slow down indeed.

Let us say that a friend of yours takes such a journey – travels in a spaceship at a speed of 186,000 miles/sec. You are both twenty years old when she leaves. Fifty years later she returns. You look around for your friend, someone you hope to recognize, even though she is now seventy years old. Instead, you see the same twenty-year-old that you said good-bye to fifty years ago. As she traveled at nearly the speed of light, time slowed down for her and for everyone and everything else on the spaceship. She aged less than a year in the time you aged fifty years. However, she does not realize time slowed down for her. She did not look in a mirror and see herself moving in slow motion. She did not check her pulse and find it beating once instead of sixty times every minute. To her, everything was normal. Everything within her frame of reference slowed down with her, making all seem normal. This phenomenon of time change at increasing speeds is known as time dilation.

We have digressed a bit from the original question – Can anything travel faster than light? We have learned that nothing can travel faster than light *in a vacuum*. But can anything travel faster than light *not* in a vacuum? Curiously, the answer is yes. In 1934 a Russian physicist, Pavel Cerenkov, speeded up electrons to 160,000 miles/sec. in water. Light in water travels at about 140,000 miles/sec. Thus, in water the electrons traveled *faster than light*! For his work, Cerenkov was awarded the Nobel Prize in physics in 1958.

Although light travels enormously fast, especially in a vacuum, it does not travel instantaneously – and this is the source of another fascinating situation. Imagine, for a moment, that you live on a planet in a galaxy so far from Earth that it takes light 100,000,000 years to reach you. (Such distant galaxies *do* exist.) Imagine also that you have a telescope powerful enough to see Earth and what is happening on Earth's surface. Would you see cars speeding on highways, people going to or from work, children at play or in school? No. You would see dinosaurs and other strange prehistoric animals roaming Earth in humid, tropical jungles. This is because it takes time for light to travel. The images that you are seeing through your telescope came from light that left Earth 100,000,000 years ago. These images are 100,000,000 years old.

That light takes time to travel can be evidenced closer to home as well. If you see the Sun rise at exactly 7:00 A.M., it actually rose at 6:52 A.M. – eight minutes earlier. It took light eight minutes to reach your eyes from the Sun. In fact, if the Sun were to suddenly explode and cease to exist, you would still see it shining quietly and steadily for eight minutes.

Light, as you can see, is a truly engrossing subject. From the simple question Can anything travel faster than light? we have converted energy into matter, slowed time, and seen dinosaurs (without having gone to Jurassic

Park!). Along the way, we even found time to answer our original question: In media such as glass or water, yes; in a vacuum, no. The speed of light in a vacuum – 186,291 miles/sec. – is the fastest that anything in the universe can travel. Sorry, Scotty!

Activities

Time to sleep it off

1 Look again at the passage. Which three things that happened to Carolina Olsson in this extract seem most unusual?

2 Imagine that you are able to interview Carolina's father. What will you ask him? What might he reply?

The stomach for the job

3 Which scenes in the story of Alexis St. Martin would make good drama? Make a list of them.

4 Imagine that you work for a television company which specializes in medical programmes. Each week there is an 'Ideas' meeting at which written proposals for programmes are discussed. Prepare a proposal that makes the case for a programme about Alexis St. Martin. Remember you have to convince the other people in your company that this will make good television.

Can anything travel faster than light?

5 Prepare quiz cards like the one below, based on what the passage tells you about light, time and speed.

Can anything travel faster than light?
a Yes.
b No.
c Yes, but only under water.

Remember to make an answer card as well.

6   You have been asked to prepare information sheets on
the subject of how fast things can move, for nine-year-
old pupils at a nearby school. Use the passage to help
you make the sheets. You need to lay the information out
in clear and interesting ways. Illustrate your sheets, if
possible; if you really can't draw, show where you would
want to have illustrations and what you would put
in them.

Overall

7   Write a two-minute piece for a radio programme called
Strange but true. Think about what sound effects you
could use, as well as what you will say. You can
dramatize your piece by including eyewitness reports if
you wish. Remember that reading something out loud
takes less time than writing it down!

Section 2
Families

We all have good and bad memories of childhood and experiences that we will never forget. It could be a visit to a relative or a strange event that sticks in our mind. In the following extracts the three writers talk about their childhood.

In 'Mukiwa' and 'Journey to my brother', the writers recall vivid events from their childhood. In Pardeep's account she tells us about her life with her family now and the problems we face as we grow older and are more aware of the way parents and older brothers and sisters get along – or don't.

Mukiwa
Peter Godwin

Peter Godwin was brought up in Rhodesia. Today Rhodesia is known as Zimbabwe. His mother was a doctor and in his book *Mukiwa* (Shona for white man) he writes about her work.

Of course, most of my mother's patients were still alive. At the African clinic on the edge of Melsetter there were hundreds of them. They lined up from early in the morning, sitting in a ragged queue that often meandered all the way down to the main road, more than eight hundred yards away. The Africans were very patient and it was an orderly queue, with no shoving or jostling for position. Just the sounds of coughing and hawking and chattering, of children crying and mothers murmuring to their babies as they breast-fed them.

The patients flocked in from the surrounding tribal lands, and they brought their own provisions with them in bundles balanced on their heads; maize cobs, sweet potatoes, mangos and bananas. And for those that hadn't, a flourishing market had grown up around the clinic's permanent queue.

The clinic itself was a small ramshackle building, easily overwhelmed by the swell of humanity that swarmed there to audition their various ailments. It consisted of two *rondavels* joined together and each topped by a conical roof of galvanized tin that gave off noises as loud as gunshots as it expanded in the sun, and again when it cooled in the late afternoon.

Every time the roof cracked, the purple-headed lizards that sunned themselves on it got a terrible fright. They scuttled desperately down the walls and slithered off into the bush. A few minutes later they returned and the whole routine would begin again. They never seemed to learn.

Janet, the nurse, lived in another double *rondavel* next door with her husband and two children. She would deal with the routine cases and keep the complicated or serious ones back for my mother to look at. Even the very serious cases would take their places patiently in the queue.

Once, when my mother was busy inside the clinic, I was playing outside with Janet's children, and I was astonished to see a man towards the end of the queue with a barbed fishing arrow straight through his head. He was sitting cross-legged, messily eating a mango with great gusto. The point of the arrow stuck out of one temple, its tail into the other.

Janet hadn't noticed him because she'd been swamped in her office processing other cases. No one else had thought to bring him to her attention. In fact no one else in the queue showed any great interest in this man who appeared to have an arrow lodged right through his brain.

I went up to say hello and he went through the whole Shona greeting rigmarole, without appearing to be in any pain.

'May I have a look?' I asked politely, as though I might have been seeking permission to inspect a piece of handiwork. He was happy to oblige and bowed his head to my level so I could examine its resident arrow. I fingered the arrowhead gingerly; the tip itself wasn't that impressive, it was very narrow, like a flattened nail, but sharp too. The impressive feature was the fearsome rows of barbs down either side of the shaft, that disappeared into a surprisingly small wound in the side of his skull.

'It is to stop the fish from escaping away,' he explained. And he launched into a learned account of the finer points of arrow fishing, which I found fascinating.

'So how did the arrow end up through your head?' I asked finally, when there was a lull in the conversation.

'It was my friend,' he said. 'My friend slipped on the mud when he was aiming the arrow.' He cocked his head to one side and laughed as though it were a minor inconvenience.

'Doesn't it hurt?' I enquired.

'No. When it first went in, it felt like a bee stinging me. But once it was inside my head, it didn't hurt too much. And my wife gave me aspirin for making headache better.' He gave his wife, who was sitting next to him, an appreciative pat and she grinned.

'Come with me,' I said. 'You should be a priority case.'

I led him to the clinic door, and called to my mother through the bead curtain that was supposed to keep the flies out of the examining room.

'Mu-um. There's a patient here that I think you should see.'

'I'm busy,' she said. 'Anyway Janet's already picked out the acute cases.'

'I think you'll want to see this chap,' I said confidently, nodding reassuringly at my companion.

I was eventually allowed to bring him in after she'd finished with her previous patient. We were delayed while I disentangled the fly beads that had got caught up on his arrow. Then we made our triumphant entrance.

My mother had her head down, writing out case notes on a filing card.

'Meet Mr Arrow Head,' I introduced.

Janet gasped and my mother looked up.

'Good God!' she spluttered.

Mr Arrow Head looked gratified that he was of such interest, and he smiled cordially as he accepted the chair Janet proffered him.

Since I had scouted him out, I was allowed to stay for the examination. They dabbed disinfectant on the entrance and exit holes, and they injected him with antibiotics and antitetanus serum. Then my mother shone her special torch into the pupils of his eyes, and did various other tests to check his reactions.

Finally she took hold of the tail end of the arrow and joggled it very tentatively. Mr Arrow Head gave a sharp intake of breath.

'Sore?' asked my mother, unnecessarily. He nodded vigorously and his arrow rotated with each nod.

'I'm afraid there's nothing more we can do for you here,' she explained to him. 'We'll order you an ambulance to take you to Umtali, and there they will x-ray you and see what to do next.'

Mr Arrow Head seemed disappointed that she wasn't going to pull the arrow out there and then.

'Will I be all right?' he asked, sounding fearful for the first time.

'Of course you will be,' said my mother. 'They've got all the latest equipment in Umtali, and I'm sure they'll take very good care of you there.'

Mr Arrow Head seemed very grateful for this reassurance, and insisted on shaking everyone's hand before leaving to sit outside on the grass once more with his wife, waiting for the ambulance to collect him.

'Remarkable!' said my mother to Janet, after he'd left. 'Absolutely extraordinary. The arrow's gone directly through his **frontal lobe** without any apparent ill effect on his **neurological activity**. Incredible.'

A few weeks later I was playing Indians in our garden before breakfast. Albert the Mozambican had helped me pitch my wigwam on the front lawn, and I was parading around barefoot on the dewy grass in a home-made cloak and a feathered head-dress, armed with my bow. I reached into my quiver for another arrow to shoot at the old gum tree when I suddenly remembered Mr Arrow Head.

Over breakfast I asked my mother what had happened to him. She continued to crunch loudly at her burnt toast, behind her newspaper, and then said through the crumbs, 'He died, of course. He never had a chance. It was a complete fluke that he lived as long as he did.'

'Well, I wish you'd told me at the time,' I grumbled.

Her newspaper came down.

'What is it now?' she asked, exasperated.

---

frontal lobe: the part of the brain which governs the nervous system
neurological activity: the reactions of the nervous system, including sensations and movement

'Nothing. It's just that if you'd told me then, I would have said goodbye to him properly.'

I got down from the table and mooched around outside for a bit. Then I fired off a couple more arrows at the old gum tree, in memory of Mr Arrow Head.

One of them was a bull's eye.

Pardeep
Sue Sharpe

In this extract Pardeep explores the nature of growing up. We notice, as we grow up, the way we and any brothers and sisters we have are treated by our parents and other relatives. How many times have you heard the words 'That's not fair – you didn't let me do that when I was that age', or 'Why doesn't he have to help do the washing up – just because he's a boy!' In some cultures boys and girls are treated differently and both boys and girls are expected to marry people within their own ethnic community. In this extract Pardeep shows us how these things can cause problems within a family.

My oldest sister had an arranged marriage, and they want us all to have one. They think they can look for the boy, make sure he's got a good job and a reasonable family, nice to talk to and that. My other sister's got a boyfriend, Joe, who's half-English and half-Indian, and she says she's happy with him. My parents don't approve of him, so she's having a really hard time. He used to be my brother's friend; she's been going out with him for two-and-a-half years, but my parents only found out nine months ago.

It's affected the way my sister gets on with my parents. They don't treat her the way she used to be treated. They turn nasty against her, and they're turning nasty against me now because I stick up for her. I say she should be allowed out, and then I get shouted at, so I'm in the middle. I think it's partly because Joe's half-white. People talk about his dad because he married a white person and my dad doesn't want people to talk about us like that. Also they think he isn't good enough for my sister because he hasn't got a steady job. They don't think he'll be able to support her. If she got married to him she'd have to work. But he's got his own market stall where he sells jackets and on a Saturday he can do about £1,000 in one day, but they don't see it like that. She said, 'You can't stop me. I love him and I want to marry him!' They plan that as soon as they've found a house they're going to get engaged. Once they're married she'll go and live with him, but until then she's staying at home.

Although my parents may get used to it I don't think they'll ever accept it, and if she married Joe she won't get as much as we will, because when you're married you get a certain amount of gold and clothes and whatever. She says it's fair enough and as long as she's happy she doesn't need anything else. She's done a beautician's course and she's thinking of opening up a salon, but if she did my parents wouldn't really help her, it would have to be her boyfriend who helps her. But they just bought my brother a new car, and they bought him the shop. He's forever getting money off them and my sister doesn't get anything. She's treated worse than the dogs because she chooses who she wants to marry. In a way it's like buying people. They give my brother so much so he'll do what they say. But my sister doesn't want to be bought, she wants them to accept her the way she is, and at the moment they don't.

I sometimes go out with my sister and Joe, but my parents – especially my mum – resent me enjoying myself with them, because at the moment my mum's cutting my sister off. Joe used to be allowed round once a week but now she doesn't even like him coming in. My brother's taken over my dad's role in the family in that when there's been festivals that Dad plays a role in, he's had to do them. But also he thinks because my dad's not here he can say that Joe can't come into the house. My mum doesn't really say anything because she doesn't want to hurt my brother, she gets really upset because she doesn't know what to do. Every time Joe phones up, it's awful if my brother picks up the phone. He'll say my sister's not in or something.

My brother's got girlfriends but because he's a boy my parents think it's all right. When he went out with this white girl, they were a bit funny about it, but they didn't really mind. I don't think it's fair. Just because we can have the babies it's like we've got to stay in and not be allowed out until we're married. They let me out to parties now, but I've got to put up a big fight about it. They say I can go out when I want, but it's only that they know I don't go out much anyway. After school I'm really tired so I tend to stay in most of the time. I did go to a party on Saturday, but I had to warn them two weeks before for that. When I ask if I can go to a party my sister says, 'Let her go out, it's only a party,' and my mum goes, 'No, she'll end up like you.'

My sisters and brother were allowed to go to parties, so it's backfired on me, and if I get a boyfriend they'll be really hurt. I do go out with boys, but I just have to keep it secret. If my parents don't approve, I can't help that: it's the way they've been brought up. But I've been brought up very different. I don't really like to lie to them, but I don't go out with lads just to get at my parents, I'll go out with them because I like them. I know it's not right, but I think I should be allowed to live my life the way I feel and not how people tell me. The worst thing was when a friend phoned up whose house I'd said I was going to, but I wasn't really, so I had to make up another lie and then I got deeper and deeper into it. I don't know what they'd do if they found out. But my parents don't seem to trust me. It's awful not to be trusted, especially by your own family, because you feel as though everything you do you're being watched. They think that as soon as I say I'm going out, I'm meeting a boy. I'll come home and they'll say, 'Where have you been? You only went to the shop, how come you've taken so long?' It's awful.

My parents think I should learn the Indian language and dress like them when I go out, and when there's any Indian functions I've got to go and be all Indian and talk to aunties that I hardly know. Then when I go to school and out with my friends, I dress the way I want. It's like being split in half, doing this for them and this for me. I just like to be me, but it's hard with parents like mine. But although it doesn't sound like it, in a way my parents give me a lot of freedom. There are girls I know that aren't allowed out at night, and not even allowed to talk to boys in the street. Although my parents are both Hindu, they're not really strict about religion, just as long as we don't go out with boys, or smoke! My brother's allowed to drink and smoke, and they don't mind my sister and I drinking with the family, but they just don't like us going out and drinking. I think in a way they're trying to be as open as they can, but they find it hard. They try to be modern, but their modern and ours are completely different.

Before my dad went to India, and before my eldest sister got married, every Sunday morning we'd all come down and have breakfast together. Then we'd just sit there and talk about relatives, and about what we're doing, where we're going, things like that. It was really relaxing and it used to make me feel secure. It was something I looked forward to. And we used to watch videos; Mum would make popcorn and if she was in a good mood she'd start telling jokes that no one found funny, but everyone laughed because it was so stupid. It used to bring us all together. As soon as my dad went, it's like something really big's gone. A big chunk of our lives disappeared.

There's times when I get really fed up. I just end up going into my room and crying all night. I can't talk to my sister because if I'm not allowed to do something, she'll say, 'Just do it, I did.' But I don't want to go behind their backs and do things. I feel quite lonely, and I've always got to have people around me because I feel really insecure. Maybe Mum's shouted at me and I've gone upstairs really upset. I think: why can't she understand the way I feel? I have anger and sympathy and everything mixed up inside, it's awful. It's all trapped up there and I think of the books I've read, and I've never read anything about emotions. I think if someone talked about them, to see how other people feel – that it's not just one person who ever feels like that – I think it would be good.

After seeing the way my sister's been treated I think I would like an arranged marriage to stay on the good side of my parents. My sister can't see it but in a way my parents are just thinking of her, seeing that she gets a nice boy and nice family background and everything, there's security there. But she wants Joe, so they're going to have to live with that. They told me it's up to me when I want to get married, but I want to get married fairly early, eighteen or so, so that I can have children so that my parents get to know their grandchildren. By the end of next year they'll be looking for a boy for me. It sounds unusual but if you've been brought up that way it's fairly natural. Parents find you a boy through word of mouth, and then you meet them. You don't have to say yes straight away, you get to go out once or twice, to get to know them. If you think it's a possibility your parents will discuss it and then you get married.

I'd like to have been able to talk openly with my mum, but it's just impossible. There's been times when I'll walk in and say something, dropping a big hint, and she'll just change the subject. She's never said anything about sex or contraception because she doesn't think I go out with boys. I think out of both my parents I get on better with my dad, but no way would I be able to talk to him about anything like that. I'm closest to my sister, but she doesn't really take me seriously enough. My parents and I used to be fairly close, but ever since they found out about Joe it's been more like two sides – my mum, dad and brother on one side and me and my sister on the other.

Journey to my brother
Leslie Thomas

Leslie Thomas spent much of his early life in a children's home as his mother had become seriously ill and eventually died. What made it worse was that he was separated without warning from his brother Roy.

For eighteen months, Leslie heard nothing about his brother. Then one day he got a letter from Roy, who was living with foster parents in a village called Long Crendon in Buckinghamshire.

Leslie made up his mind immediately: 'I knew I would have to see him again.' This is what happened when he ran away in order to try to find his brother.

The journey to my brother lasted about five days. I walked a good part of the way, resting away from the road every so often in a field or a lane. Twice I got good long lifts, once on a lorry and once in a van, but the driver of the van misunderstood the place I wanted to go and I went miles astray.

He did not ask me where I had come from, nor did he seem to need to know anything else about me. He was a young man in blue overalls, and he whistled through his teeth all the time we were travelling.

Then when the lorry stopped the driver had a big bundle of a dog in the cab. 'If you want a lift you'll have to get on the back,' he said. Then he laughed and called after me: 'That's if you can stand it.'

I climbed on to the back of the lorry and I understood what he meant. He had been around the countryside collecting swill for pigs. There were six or seven bins full of it and it slopped and flopped over the side as the road bent and the lorry jumped. The smell unfurled behind the bins, fluttering like a banner, and although I crouched right on the tailboard, with my head hanging over the side, I could still not avoid it.

At nights, during the journey, I slept twice under bridges; once under a railway bridge and once under a bridge across a river with a small path where the arch and water touched. There was a leaf-shaped boat pulled up on the path and a tarpaulin in the boat. I lay in the boat, and it rained outside the bridge and the rain slipped off the arch and into the river making a noise like a waterfall. Even when the rain stopped I couldn't sleep because it dripped into the river all night.

On the other two nights I slept in country bus shelters, on the benches, with my collar pulled right up and my face turned away from the road so that it would not show up white to anyone passing.

It was strange, for no one bothered me all the time I was on my way. You might have thought that a boy in a deformed blue suit, with a yellow tie, yellow gloves and a music case, might have attracted some curiosity, but I did not. I made sure that I did not look too vagabond by carefully washing in a stream or river as soon as I could each day, combing my hair and trying to keep my shirt and tie straight.

Before I had set out the thought that worried me most was that I might get so hungry that I would have to give myself up. But on the road I had no anxiety because there were orchards still **bushelled** with fruit, and it lay clustered in the autumn grass under the hedgerows. There were still blackberrries in the thorns, and I

---

bushelled: heavy (a bushel is an old form of measurement used for dry goods: 1 bushel is 36.37 litres)

collected ears of wheat, left lying in open fields after the harvesting, and munched it as I went.

In Wendover I bought a loaf of bread from a woman in a baker's shop who looked at me in a strange way, and I bought a couple of buns the next day from another place.

It was a fine journey really. It did not rain very much in the day and although I got tired I was never sad. I found that if you did not think of the steps you were pacing, or count the miles too diligently, the places you aimed for seemed to arrive so quickly that they might have set out themselves to meet you half-way.

There was plenty to see and think about. There were grey and red houses sitting like resting travellers at the roadside and others by themselves up on the brows of the gentle Chilterns. I wondered why people should build houses like that, away and alone, with a valley and perhaps a wood between them and their neighbours. I would see a house like that, and imagine the man going gladly home in the evening and sitting out in front for a while and watching anything that was going on below. Or perhaps just sitting and watching nothing in particular but the light going off fields and the late sky and the dull shining of a river or stream.

Two of the afternoons turned warm and I got dusty and dry as I walked. My toes were uncomfortable too because my shoes were a bit small and my toes were always a funny collection anyway, all pushed and bunched together like people in a bus.

Autumn showed most in the trees. Where they stood together in woods or copses they were like girls standing together, each girl with a different colour hair.

Some of the fields were already turned and tilled, brown and vacant, with birds sitting on the furrows.

Sometimes, as I went, I would think about words. Not in any context or sentence, not in any poem or rhyme. But words for themselves alone, for what they were, simple and coloured and fine, each one a poem or a picture.

Fall for autumn, sorrel for a horse, burnished for what the trees were. Just words. Lonely, loftily, topsail, reef, mist, oleander, isthmus, seascape, widgeon, conifer, quadrille, wild and wanderlust. Largo in music, sonnet in readings, Curaçao, Cayenne and Lourenço Marques for places that were far away.

Once, at the roadside, there was a timbered cottage alongside a stone wall, like an old ship lying at a jetty.

The roof had sighed and sagged in the middle and moss and ivy lived on the walls and windowsills. It looked, I thought then, the sort of house that had wanted lots of things doing to it for years; a comfortable house, a place where the man never quite got around to getting things done. The garden was a nice, random affair too, as though he had put the flowers and the plants in the piece of ground that happened to be nearest his hand at the time. He had not even bothered to take the deck chair in from the grass. It had been out all the summer, you could tell that by its faded face. Now the rain had soaked it and it nursed dying leaves in its lap.

At home, at home with my mother I mean, we had always *tried* to have a garden. I had worked hard in it but somehow it had never grown. In the front garden there was the infirm climber clinging desperately to the brick wall, and this my mother always referred to as 'the dog rose tree'. We also had some irises which appeared like a miracle every year, some jungled grass and a privet hedge. In the middle of the grass I had once cut and dug a rectangular flower bed, but the pink, fluffy woman who used to come to tea and tell my mother's fortune saw it and leaned over to me and said: 'It shouldn't be there, boy. It looks just like a grave.'

Terrified, I replaced all the turves of grass I had removed and then it looked more like a grave than ever. So I pulled them up again and frantically dug the whole garden over. After that it rained and the place became a morass.

At the back the garden was a bit longer, starting at the kitchen door and terminating at the boards that fenced us off from the engine sheds. Every spring I dug the thick ground and planted potatoes and lettuces and dwarf beans, and some of them grew.

The man next door gave me some strawberry plants and they produced three strawberries in the summer of 1942. My brother ate all three at one go and I got him on the ground and punched him until my mother came out and pulled us apart.

When we heard that the Government were going to provide us with air-raid shelters I dug a substantial hole at the bottom of the garden to receive ours, imagining at every exhausting spadeful that this was my war effort. Then some men came along, dug another hole at the top of the garden and placed the air-raid shelter in it. My hole remained there forever, a wadi in summer, a pool in the rains, and a place for drifting snow in the deep of winter.

As I walked towards Long Crendon, through the strange countryside and the unknown towns, I wondered how Roy would look now. It was a year and a half since I had stumbled from the ambulance with the woman promising that I would see him again the next day, and left him sitting up puzzled on the stretcher, with his small bundle of belongings on the floor.

It was in the late afternoon that I saw my first signpost with 'Long Crendon' on it. I was tired and there was a wind walking about in the trees; an autumn wind throwing birds and clouds about in the sky and singing a song of a cold night to come.

Long Crendon, said the signpost, was ten miles.
Walking, weary as I now was, I knew I would never get
there that night. It meant sleeping once more in some
rough place, cold and aching and afraid again, listening
for footsteps and watching for headlights on the road.

I walked for about half a mile up the road which went
from the signpost.

Then I stopped, and stood in the hedge for a while
and watched a police car parked two hundred yards
farther on. Presently a policeman appeared, turned the
car around and drove off in the other direction. I went
cautiously along through the briars and the ditches and
came opposite the place where the car had been. It was
a country police station, a house really, with a yard, a
notice board, and a garage.

For a moment I had a suspicious, and thrilling, feeling
that my picture might be on the notice board with the word
'Wanted' above it, and a full description, down to my yellow
tie and my banana gloves, beneath. But there was no notice
and nobody seemed to be about either, just the wind
sweeping the yard and brushing the hedges and boughs.

At the moment when I was about to walk on, giving
myself a mental warning to keep a watch for the police car
returning, I noticed a shed at the side of the yard. Its roof
slid low and it was open at the front. Inside were half a
dozen bicycles.

It was a few strides across the yard. I took the bike that
came first, which was also the oldest and most cranky, this
being some saver for my conscience.

I ran with it across the yard and out into the road
where I mounted it. It worked. It went. Apart from a
tendency for the saddle to slip from side to side with each
movement of the legs, it worked and went fine.

Joyously now I rode, my music case hanging from the
handlebars, the old bike going along like a charger

suddenly freed from a stable. I knew the wind was with me for I could feel it pushing behind my ears, and pummelling my back, and the grey clouds raced along above me like a hunting pack.

Once the music case slipped and fell on to the road, the tin of toffees inside it clanging as it hit the ground. The bike had no working brakes, I discovered at that moment, and I had to scrape along with my feet before I could stop it. Then, a few minutes later, a car rounded a curve far ahead and, thinking it was the homing police car, I swerved the bike recklessly from the road, collided with a gate and completed the spectacular movement by somersaulting from the saddle into the field.

The car went past without stopping and I was crouching in the hedge at that time, so I did not know whether it was the police car or not.

I pushed off again, the way the clouds were running. The figures on the signposts diminished. At last there was one which said 'Long Crendon 1 mile'.

It was evening everywhere now, broken clouds over broken fields, with the trees becoming smudgy and merged, early lights in far windows and smoke curling like locks of dark hair. The road led straight into the village. I had never been there before and I never went there again, but I remember a big field with a low wall skirting it, and the road running along by the wall.

My brother was walking across the field, diagonally towards the road, as I pedalled along by the wall. Even though there was dusk and a year and a half between us, I knew it was Roy.

'Roy! Roy! Roy! Roy!' I don't know how many times I called, or why I kept calling like that, because he heard me first time and he knew it was me because he cried back and raced towards the gate in the wall.

He was running and I was pedalling, and I got there first, but the bike was going at such a pace that it slid beneath me and careered on as I jumped off. I fell over, then got up again, just as he was running to the gate.

He was not much different really, a bit taller, but skinny still, and grinning with his broken tooth at the front, and his hair straight down over his eyes. He climbed on the gate and dropped over.

We just stood, facing each other, neither of us knowing what to do next. My instinct was to put my arms around him because he was my brother and I loved him dearly, but boys don't do that sort of thing easily. And it seemed too formal, too grown up, to shake hands. That would have been just as foolish.

So I said: ''lo Roy.'

''ello Les,' he said.

'Here,' I said, fumbling in my music case. 'I've got some toffees for you.'

Because they had not liked his name, his foster parents called him George. This made me angry at the time, and still does. It was not sufficient that he, at nine years of age, should suddenly be taken from everything he knew, but after going through the pipeline of the system he should find himself with a new name.

His foster parents were kind country people with a small house where they made me a bed on the landing. But to them he was George, and at school he was George. It reeked of injustice to me. Roy, after all, was good enough for his first mother.

I sat on the end of his bed for hours that night and we talked quietly like two mice. Talked of all the days we had known together, and the days since, and all that had happened. He had been the most unhappy after we had been parted, and he kept writing letters to our mother and getting no reply. When the Martin family went to see him and told him that she had been dead for a year he had cried, but felt relieved in an odd way too, because he had thought that she did not want to have anything to do with him any more.

He was content now in this small place. It was strange to hear him call the woman in the house Mum, and to hear him say that his father was a thatcher. He talked of villages around the countryside, and boys at school, and summer cricket matches, and how they had been down to Marlow and the Thames for a holiday. All the things we had known, the lamp-post games on winter nights, the dusty street in August, the Ebbw coal we cut from the black river bank, our friends and foes, our parents and the big black and white cat, were all of a different time and a different place, and would never be ours again.

But he was no stranger to me, nor I to him. For this I was happy and thankful. I had often wondered if he would still be my brother when I found him again. And he was.

On the following day I took the bike from the front door and returned the way I had come. Roy's foster parents did not ask me how I had made the journey, and I did not tell them, nor him.

Roy walked down to the wall and the gate with me. We knew that we would never lose each other again. He climbed on the wall and waved as I went away, and he was still waving as I turned the bend in the road and left the village behind.

Easily now I pedalled back to the police station, swerved into the yard spectacularly, and replaced the cycle in the little shed with the others. I am certain that no one ever knew it was missing, certainly no one mentioned it to me.

I went to the door of the police station and gave myself up. A surprised-looking policeman with no helmet, and a cup of coffee in his hand, saw me standing there.

'I'm wanted by the police,' I said dramatically.

'Oh are you,' he said, taking a drink of coffee. 'Well it looks like we've found you, don't it.'

Actually he'd never heard of me, which was a bit disappointing, but I had a fine lunch there, and a good tea in the afternoon, before they took me back to Dickies in a police car.

I was apprehensive as the journey was getting towards its end. After all I had been away nearly a week and the Gaffer had been known to be tough about things like that. But at the door of Dickies one of the staff matrons accepted me, and sent me upstairs for a bath. She said hardly anything at all and after I had bathed I was told to go to bed.

Activities

Mukiwa

1   Write down five things that you remember about this story. Leave a few lines between each.

    Now go back to each and try to add more detail by looking more closely at the story.

2   Imagine that you are going to turn this story into a play. Write the script for this episode of Peter's life story.

    Write the dialogue the actors and actresses would use. Look at the conversations in the passage to help you, and think about how the characters might say the lines.

Pardeep

3   What do you learn about the individual members of this family? Make a list of the family members and write as much as you can about each.

    You may wish to discuss possible answers to the next questions with a partner before you write them down.

4   These parents treat their children differently. What do you think of this?

5   What do you think of the behaviour of the brother?

6   What do you think of arranged marriages? Can you think of some advantages and disadvantages?

Journey to my brother

7   On page 35 Les says that Roy kept writing letters to their mother and getting no reply. Imagine you are Roy. Write one of the letters to your mother. You may want to include information about what you have been doing, as well as asking questions about both her and your brother.

8   Imagine that you are Les. Write a letter to your friend
         telling him/her about your journey, how you felt when
         you found your brother and how you felt afterwards
         when you left him again.

Overall

9   You have been asked to prepare a magazine article
         entitled 'The best thing about my family is . . .'

         The idea is that the article will feature several families
         and their views. Talk to three or four people about their
         families. Once you have collected what different people
         have to say, you will need to think carefully about how
         to present it.

Section 3
Pages from a diary

Diaries can be very private affairs: they contain the sort of things that would make you crawl into a corner and wish you were dead if your parents read them. That may be the usual situation, but it is not always like that. Every now and then, a person uses the diary format to let other people understand what life has been like for them. That is the case with the three writers gathered together here. Each one of them wants to communicate what life was like in the times they are describing.

Accident
Arno Bo

Rosemyn Bo's story has been written up for her in diary form by her father. Rosemyn was nine years old at the time of these events. It all starts with an early departure from a family birthday party . . .

Sunday, December 13th

We've played with the kittens for an hour. Phoebe is crazy about them. She wants to hug them all the time and have them on her lap.

Leon won't play with us. He's seventeen today and too grown up, of course. He's our cousin, but I wish he were my brother. The kittens belong to my other cousins: Elise and Rachel.

We've had Coke and crisps, and I think I can smell sausage rolls in the oven, but no, we are going home because Dad has had the flu and he doesn't feel too well.

Anyway, the kittens have just jumped through their catdoor into the garage, and Mum is coming out. My mother is the dearest and most beautiful Mum in the world: she has goldish hair and big, honest eyes that always know everything. She talks to Aunt Laura while Dad waits impatiently in the car. Then we drive away.

It's pitch dark tonight. Next week will be the shortest day of the year – all cosy and snug. I always turn on the lights early and draw the curtains. Then we have hot chocolate. And a hot-water bottle in bed.

The road is very quiet and it's also quiet in the car; we are all tired – just staring into the blackness. It's drizzling.

Monday tomorrow. I hate school. But it's Christmas next week. I'm going to sing in the choir, on stage! And Phoebe is going to be an angel.

I'm sitting behind Mum, leaning on the front seat – a good place to suck my thumb and watch the road, to see everything.

Sometimes I see more than Dad, because I don't have to steer. Now and then he looks at me in the mirror and we wink at each other.

It's pretty boring outside because . . .

'Hey, watch out, Dad!'

What is he doing? Look in front of you, Dad!

There is a bend in the road but he doesn't steer round it, he keeps on going straight . . .

We hit something and are all thrown about. It hurts and I feel sick.

Dad turns the wheel wildly now. What's he doing? I want to help, to scream, to crawl away, but I feel like lead. I can't do anything.

The world is falling over me. I'm lost.

Silence. Darkness.

There was a bang. Right through me. I still feel it. Where am I?

It's so dark and silent.

Pain.

Inside me the banging goes on. Where are we?

Still in the car.

I want to get out but I can't move. I'm stuck. Nobody moves. If only this pain would go away.

How long have we been there?

Somebody is coming. She looks into the car.

'What's your name?' she asks.

'Rosemyn.'

'And your sister?'

'Phoebe.'

'We've called for help. They'll be here very soon.'

She is holding my hand.

'My arm hurts,' I say. 'Has this really happened?'

Something bad must have happened.

Phoebe has fallen forward and her head is funny. She isn't moving. Where are Mum and Dad? It's so dark. The woman puts Phoebe's head straight. Then Phe throws up. But she doesn't say anything and her eyes are closed.

I hear sirens. There are people everywhere. They are all talking at once and running up and down.

A window is taken out of the car. Cold. Slowly they move something and I am lifted out. My arm still hurts.

Now a man is holding me.

'How old are you?' he asks.

'Nine.'

'When are you going to be ten?'

'In August.'

'And how old is your sister?'

'Six.'

He says: 'I have two daughters myself.'

'Not to the hospital, not to the hospital,' I say.

The sirens and lights are everywhere.

'I don't want an injection.'

Who are they? What are they doing? All these people – there must be a hundred, running and talking anxiously . . .

A huge lamp is turned on. I shut my eyes.

Has this really happened?

Someone puts me down. Then I am lifted into a big car.

'Don't take me to the hospital. No!'

'What's your name?' asks another man.

'Where do you live?'

'Which school do you go to?'

But I can see blood.

'Please don't talk about it,' I say. 'It's horrible . . .'

'I'm going to give you an injection,' says the man. 'Everything will be all right. We'll take good care of you.'

He stays beside me all the time. I'm so tired. It's an ambulance and I've never been so tired.

'Blood on the floor . . . Don't talk about it.'

Why is it taking so long? Where are Mum and Dad, and Phoebe?

Drive slowly, I want to say, we've just had an accident.

He seems to be driving very fast.

I'd like to sleep, but that is frightening too.

*

I'm in the hospital.

The others are injured too. That's why nobody's come to take me home.

Doctors and nurses keep coming in to examine me. They tell me what happened: we crashed into a tree. It was a serious accident. These words stick in my head.

There are pieces of glass in my face; they are taken out. I don't really notice how much it hurts.

Photos are taken that show everywhere in my body: X-rays. My arm is broken in a difficult spot, near my shoulder. A nurse stays with me and she gives me a little white felt dog.

Luckily I can still suck my thumb. It's my other arm they put in a sling.

What are we waiting for now?

The door opens and Gran and Grandad come in. Why are they here?

'We crashed! I *told* Dad: "Watch out!"'

They know. That's why they are here, because Mum and Dad are injured.

Mum is in a different hospital, in Denton.

'Why isn't she here?' I ask.

'It's difficult for a hospital to handle four casualties at the same time, especially on a Sunday.'

She'll be all right, of course. That's what hospitals are for. The man said so. But when are we going to see Mum? And when are we going home?

Gran and Grandad are talking with the doctors. Uncle John and Aunt Laura have come now.

I watch their faces and then I'm not so sure . . . Will it really be all right?

'What has happened to Mum?'

'She's quite badly hurt, mostly to her head and stomach. It's rather serious, I'm afraid.'

'How?'

'She is too ill to be moved.'

I want to ask more but I don't dare.

'And Phoebe?'

'She has a kind of concussion.'

'And Dad?'

'A broken leg and something wrong with his chest.'

They are careful, trying not to talk, not to be sad.

'What *I've* got is worst, isn't it?'

(Why do I ask that? I just *hope* what I've got is worst.)

'Well . . .' Aunt Laura begins.

I say quickly: 'It's Dad's fault. He's the one who crashed.'

'But not on purpose, my sweet. No one does these things on purpose.'

I try not to think any more. But thoughts keep coming: it's Dad's fault and Mum is all by herself, in a hospital that is much too big and much too far away.

I'm taken to a different department.

They have to do something to my arm and a nurse says: 'This will hurt a bit.'

It does. But other things are more important.

They bring a special bed, because my arm has to be hung from a frame: a traction. Uncle John helps; he is so clever.

What a stupid thing! I can hardly move, and I'm not allowed to, otherwise my arm won't heal.

Just so long as Mum gets better.

People look so . . . so strange. I'm being quite normal – on the outside – but I'm afraid to look at them.

Mum was so pretty tonight, with her new cardigan and lovely little boots. I hope they aren't lost. I'd like to touch the fur of the boots now. I want to touch my Mum.

*

A nurse has come to say that Dad was operated on. He is on a different floor – unconscious.

Gran and Grandad are allowed to see him.

And Phoebe? She is in the other ward too – it's called Intensive Care, for people who are very ill – and she is also unconscious. Luckily they can do anything in a hospital. But it's a shame they are so far away.

Where am I going to sleep?

They take me to 6 East. That's the children's ward, on the sixth floor.

Saturday, December 19th

At first, Phoebe is still crying and screaming in her sleep. At six o'clock they give her some food through the tube and now she is calm.

'Phe?'

She looks at me but doesn't say anything.

'Shall I sing to you?'

She smiles and that's the sweetest thing I've ever seen. I sing a few songs I happen to think of, about summer and winter, and about Christmas.

They are going to take me to Dad and I can't wait! After a day like yesterday it seems we haven't seen each other for weeks. Surely *he* knows how Mum is.

They wheel my bed in, next to Dad's.

'Hey,' I say, 'have you got a telephone?'

Stupid question, but I'm so nervous.

'Yes,' he says, *'very* useful.'

Have you called Denton yet? I should be asking.

I look around and think of all kinds of things, as if I'm dizzy, as if I'm floating everywhere at the same time . . . *What* are we saying?

Suddenly I hear Dad's voice: 'Mum is not going to get better. She is going to die. She will go back to heaven, to the light.'

From very far away I fall back into my bed, beside Dad, who looks horribly tired.

Mum is going to die.

He has said it.

My mother?

Not on television, not in a book. Our own, real Mum will never come home again.

What about us?

'No! Mum is not going to die! I don't *want* her to. And you can never be sure. Then why did you cause the accident?'

'I didn't. I mean, not on purpose. An accident *happens*.'

'Mum doesn't want to die either, because if she did we wouldn't have a mother.'

'Yes, for your sake Mum doesn't want to die. Perhaps that's why it's taking so long. But her body is all broken . . .'

'What's wrong with her then?'

'Her brain is partly dead already. If she were to live, she might not be able to walk, or talk. She must continue on her way and that way is now leading to heaven. Which is really a good thing for her.'

'But not for us.'

'No. For us it's hard. And Mum *knows* it. That's terrible for her as well.'

'So you don't know for sure that she is going to die.'

'No, I *think* so. We must wait and get strong. And inside you can always talk with Mum.'

It is never certain. Miracles happen, don't they? But . . .

Now I know what I've seen in all those eyes. I knew it from the beginning!

We are both crying.

I can't crawl into Dad's lap and we can't lean against each other.

Holding my hand, he tries to get that pretty box of tissues and give it to me. He can't, the box is too far away, on his night table, but he does it all the same!

After that he collapses again. It hurt too much. Still, I suddenly think he's strong, like Gran said the other day. He's so quiet, I mean . . . not just because he's tired.

I'm even relieved. At least he has said it! Although I don't want to believe what I know.

Knee-deep in glass
Zlata Filipovic

Zlata Filipovic was eleven, two years older than Rosemyn, when she began to write down what it was like to live in Sarajevo. It was 1992 and the Serbs had begun to attack. Zlata knew little or nothing the politics that was turning a once beautiful city into a war zone. All she knew was the effect it had on the daily lives of her family and friends. She gave her diary a name – Mimmy – so she could write in it in the same way as she would write to a best friend.

Saturday, 2 May 1992

Dear Mimmy,
Today was truly, absolutely the worst day ever in Sarajevo. The shooting started around noon. Mummy and I moved into the hall. Daddy was in his office, under our flat, at the time. We told him on the interphone to run quickly to the downstairs lobby where we'd meet him. We brought Cicko [Zlata's canary] with us. The gunfire was getting worse, and we couldn't get over the wall to the Bobars', so we ran down to our own cellar.

The cellar is ugly, dark, smelly. Mummy, who's terrified of mice, had two fears to cope with. The three of us were in the same corner as the other day. We listened to the pounding shells, the shooting, the thundering noise overhead. We even heard planes. At one moment I realized that this awful cellar was the only place that could save our lives. Suddenly, it started to look almost warm and nice. It was the only way we could defend ourselves against all this terrible shooting. We heard glass shattering in our street. Horrible. I put my fingers in my ears to block out the terrible sounds. I was worried about Cicko. We had left him behind in the lobby. Would he catch cold there? Would something hit him? I was terribly hungry and thirsty. We had left our half-cooked lunch in the kitchen.

When the shooting died down a bit, Daddy ran over to our flat and brought us back some sandwiches. He said he could smell something burning and that the phones weren't working. He brought our TV set down to the cellar. That's when we learned that the main post office (near us) was on fire and that they had kidnapped our President. At around 20.00 we went back up to our flat. Almost every window in our street was broken. Ours were all right, thank God. I saw the post office in flames. A terrible sight. The fire-fighters battled with the raging fire. Daddy took a few photos of the post office being devoured by the flames. He said they wouldn't come out because I had been fiddling with something on the camera. I was sorry. The whole flat smelled of the burning fire. God, and I used to pass by there every day. It had just been done up. It was huge and beautiful, and now it was being swallowed up by the flames. It was disappearing. That's what this neighbourhood of mine looks like, dear Mimmy. I wonder what it's like in other parts of town? I heard on the radio that it was awful around the Eternal Flame. The place is knee-deep in glass. We're worried about Grandma and Grandad. They live there. Tomorrow, if we can go out, we'll see how they are. A terrible day. This has been the worst, most awful day in my eleven-year-old life. I hope it will be the only one.

Mummy and Daddy are very edgy. I have to go to bed. Ciao!
Zlata

*

Sunday, 3 May 1992

Dear Mimmy,
Daddy managed to run across the bridge over the Miljacka and get to Grandma and Grandad. He came running back, all upset, sweating with fear and sadness. They're all right, thank God. Tito Street looks awful. The heavy shelling has destroyed shop windows, cars, flats, the fronts and roofs of buildings. Luckily, not too many people were hurt because they managed to take shelter. Neda (Mummy's girlfriend) rushed over to see how we were and to tell us that they were OK and hadn't had any damage. But it was terrible.

We talked through the window with Auntie Boda and Bojana just now. They were in the street yesterday when that heavy shooting broke out. They managed to get to Stela's cellar.
Zlata

Tuesday, 5 May 1992

Dear Mimmy,
The shooting seems to be dying down. I guess they've caused enough misery, although I don't know why. It has something to do with politics. I just hope the 'kids' come to some agreement. Oh, if only they would, so we could live and breathe as human beings again. The things that have happened here these past few days are terrible. I want it to stop for ever. PEACE! PEACE!

I didn't tell you, Mimmy, that we've rearranged things in the flat. My room and Mummy's and Daddy's are too dangerous to be in. They face the hills, which is where they're shooting from. If only you knew how scared I am to go near the windows and into those rooms. So, we

turned a safe corner of the sitting room into a 'bedroom'. We sleep on mattresses on the floor. It's strange and awful. But, it's safer that way. We've turned everything around for safety. We put Cicko in the kitchen. He's safe there, although once the shooting starts there's nowhere safe except the cellar. I suppose all this will stop and we'll all go back to our usual places.
Ciao!
Zlata

Thursday, 7 May 1992

Dear Mimmy,
I was almost positive the war would stop, but today . . . Today a shell fell on the park in front of my house, the park where I used to play with my girlfriends. A lot of people were hurt. From what I hear Jaca, Jaca's mother, Selma, Nina, our neighbour Dado and who knows how many other people who happened to be there were wounded. Dado, Jaca and her mother have come home from hospital, Selma lost a kidney but I don't know how she is, because she's still in hospital. AND NINA IS DEAD. A piece of shrapnel lodged in her brain and she died. She was such a sweet, nice little girl. We went to kindergarten together, and we used to play together in the park. Is it possible I'll never see Nina again? Nina, an innocent eleven-year-old little girl – the victim of a stupid war. I feel sad. I cry and wonder why? She didn't do anything. A disgusting war has destroyed a young child's life. Nina, I'll always remember you as a wonderful little girl.
Love, Mimmy,
Zlata

*

Wednesday, 13 May 1992

Dear Mimmy,
Life goes on. The past is cruel, and that's exactly why we should forget it.

The present is cruel too and I can't forget it. There's no joking with war. My present reality is the cellar, fear, shells, fire.

Terrible shooting broke out the night before last. We were afraid that we might be hit by shrapnel or a bullet, so we ran over to the Bobars'. We spent all of that night, the next day and the next night in the cellar and in Nedo's flat. (Nedo is a refugee from Grbavica. He left his parents and came here to his sister's empty flat.) We saw terrible scenes on TV. The town in ruins, burning, people and children being killed. It's unbelievable.

The phones aren't working, we haven't been able to find out anything about Grandma and Grandad, Melica, how people in other parts of town are doing. On TV we saw the place where Mummy works, Vodoprivreda, all in flames. It's on the aggressor's side of town (Grbavica). Mummy cried. She's depressed. All her years of work and effort – up in flames. It's really horrible. All around Vodoprivreda there were cars burning, people dying, and nobody could help them. God, why is this happening?

I'M SO MAD I WANT TO SCREAM AND BREAK EVERYTHING!
Your Zlata

Thursday, 14 May 1992

Dear Mimmy,
The shelling here has stopped. Daddy managed to run over to Grandma's and Grandad's to see how they are,

how they've been coping with the madness of the past few days. They're all right, thank God. Melica and her family are all right, and Grandma heard from Vinko that Meda and Bojan (an aunt and her son) are also all right.

The situation at the Marshal Tito barracks and in the new parts of town is terrible. It's a madhouse around the electricity board building and the radio and television centre. I can't watch television any more. I can't bear to. The area around Otes seems to be the only place that is still quiet. Mummy's brother Braco and his family live there. They're so lucky, there's no shooting where they live.
Zlata

Sunday, 17 May 1992

Dear Mimmy,
It's now definite: there's no more school. The war has interrupted our lessons, closed down the schools, sent children to cellars instead of classrooms. They'll give us the grades we got at the end of last term. So I'll get a report card saying I've finished fifth grade.
Ciao!
Zlata

Wednesday, 20 May 1992

Dear Mimmy,
The shooting has died down. Today Mummy felt brave enough to cross the bridge. She saw Grandma and Grandad, ran into various people she knows and heard a lot of sad news. She came back all miserable. Her brother was wounded on 14 May, driving home from work. Her brother is hurt and she doesn't find out about it until

today – that's terrible. He was wounded in the leg and is in hospital. How can she get to him? It's like being at the other end of the world now. They told her he's all right, but she doesn't believe them and keeps crying. If only the shooting would stop, she could go to the hospital. She says: 'I won't believe it until I see him with my own eyes.'
Zlata

Thursday, 21 May 1992

Dear Mimmy,
Mummy went to see Braco in the hospital today. He's alive. That's the most important thing. But he's badly wounded. It's his knee. Two hundred wounded were brought to the clinic that day. They were going to amputate his leg, but his friend Dr Adnan Dizdar (the surgeon) recognized him, cancelled the amputation and took him into the operating theatre. The operation lasted four-and-a-half hours and the doctors say it was a success. But he'll have to stay in bed for a long, long time. He has some rods, a cast, all sorts of things on his leg. Mummy is terribly worried and sad. So are Grandma and Grandad (that's what Mummy tells me, because I haven't seen them since 12 April; I haven't been out of the house). In the end he was lucky. I hope it will turn out all right. Hold on there, Braco!!!
Your Zlata

Saturday, 23 May 1992

Dear Mimmy,
I'm not writing to you about me any more. I'm writing to you about war, death, injuries, shells, sadness and sorrow.

Almost all my friends have left. Even if they were here, who knows whether we'd be able to see each other. The phones aren't working, we couldn't even talk to each other. Vanja and Andrej have gone to join Srdjan in Dubrovnik. The war has stopped there. They're lucky. I was so unhappy because of that war in Dubrovnik. I never dreamed it would move to Sarajevo. Verica and Bojana have also left.

I now spend all my time with Bojana and Maja. They're my best friends now. Bojana is a year-and-a-half older than me, she's finished seventh grade and we have a lot in common. Maja is in her last year of school. She's much older than I am, but she's wonderful. I'm lucky to have them, otherwise I'd be all alone among the grown-ups.

On the news they reported the death of Silva Rizvanbegović, a doctor at the Emergency Clinic, who's Mummy's friend. She was in an ambulance. They were driving a wounded man to get him help. Lots of people Mummy and Daddy know have been killed. Oh, God, what is happening here???

Love,
Zlata

Through a glass darkly
Jean-Dominique Bauby

Jean-Dominique Bauby had a pleasant and comfortable life in Paris with his family until one Friday in December 1995. On that day, he had a massive stroke. Even a few years ago, he would simply have died. Instead, they were able to keep him alive, but at a price. His brain worked but almost nothing else. He was paralysed from head to toe. The only thing he could do for himself was to blink his left eyelid. Incredibly, he was able to work out a way of communicating. The book he dictated is a kind of diary, recording his feelings and experiences on various days. Here is just one section.

Hunched in my wheelchair, I surreptitiously watch my children as their mother pushes me down the hospital corridor. While I have become something of a zombie father, Théophile and Céleste are very much flesh and blood, energetic and noisy. I will never tire of seeing them walk alongside me, just walking, their confident expressions masking the unease weighing on their small shoulders. As he walks, Théophile dabs with a Kleenex at the thread of saliva escaping my closed lips. His movements are tentative, at once tender and fearful, as if he were dealing with an unpredictable animal. As soon as we slow down, Céleste cradles my head in her bare arms, covers my forehead with noisy kisses and says over and over, 'You're my dad, you're my dad,' as if in incantation.

Today is Father's Day. Until my stroke we had felt no need to fit this made-up holiday into our emotional calendar. But this time we spent the whole of this symbolic day together, affirming that even a rough sketch, a shadow, a tiny fragment of a dad is still a dad. I am torn between joy at seeing them living, moving, laughing or crying for a few hours, and fear that the sight of all these sufferings – beginning with mine – is not the ideal entertainment for a boy of ten and his eight-year-old sister. However, we have made the wise collective decision not to sugarcoat anything.

We install ourselves at the Beach Club – my name for a patch of sand-dune open to sun and wind, where the hospital has obligingly set out tables, chairs and umbrellas, and even planted a few buttercups which grow in the sand amid the weeds. In this neutral zone on the beach, a transition between hospital and everyday life, one could easily imagine some good fairy turning every wheelchair into a chariot. 'Want to play hangman?' asks Théophile, and I ache to tell him that I have enough on my plate playing quadriplegic. But my communication system disqualifies repartee: the keenest rapier grows dull and falls flat when it takes several minutes to thrust it home. By the time you strike, even you no longer understand what had seemed so witty before you started to dictate it, letter by letter. So the rule is to avoid impulsive sallies. It deprives conversation of its sparkle, all those gems you bat back and forth like a ball – and I count this forced lack of humour one of the great drawbacks of my condition.

But we can certainly play hangman, the national pre-teen sport. I guess a letter, then another, then stumble on the third. My heart is not in the game. Grief surges over me. His face not two feet from mine, my son Théophile sits patiently waiting – and I, his father, have lost the simple right to ruffle his bristly hair, clasp his downy neck, hug his small, lithe, warm body tight against me. There are no words to express it. My condition is monstrous, iniquitous, revolting, horrible. Suddenly I can take no more. Tears well and my throat emits a hoarse rattle that startles Théophile. Don't be scared, little man, I love you. Still engrossed in the game, he moves in for the kill. Two more letters: he has won, and I have lost. On a corner of the page he completes his drawing of the gallows, the rope and the condemned man.

Meanwhile, Céleste is doing cartwheels on the sand. Perhaps some compensatory mechanism is at work, for ever since the act of blinking became the equivalent of weightlifting for me she has turned into a genuine acrobat. With the flexibility of a cat she does a backflip, a handstand, a somersault and a whole series of daring leaps and twists. She has recently added tight-rope walker to the long list of professions she envisages for the future (after schoolteacher, super-model and florist). With the onlookers at the Beach Club won over by her display, our budding entertainer now launches into a song-and-dance act, to the great dismay of Théophile, who more than anything hates drawing attention to himself. As shy and reclusive as his sister is outgoing, he wholeheartedly hated me the day I sought and obtained permission to ring the school bell for the first day of class. No one can predict whether Théophile will be happy: but it is certain that he will live in the shadows.

I wonder how Céleste has managed to accumulate such a repertoire of Sixties songs, Johnny Hallyday, Sylvie Vartan, Sheila, Clo-Clo, Françoise Hardy – all the stars of that golden era. Alongside universally familiar numbers, Céleste sings forgotten hits that trail clouds of nostalgia in their wake. Not since I was twelve, when I endlessly played it on my record-player, have I heard the Clo-Clo François 45 rpm 'Poor Little Rich Girl'. Yet as soon as Céleste begins it – somewhat off-key – every note, every verse, every detail of back-up and orchestration comes back to me with startling precision, right down to the sound of the sea that filters through the opening bars. Once again I see the album cover, the singer's photo, his striped button-down shirt. I longed for a shirt like his, but for me it was unattainable: my mother considered it tacky. I even relive the Saturday afternoon when I bought the record. My father's cousin kept a tiny record shop in the lower level of the Gare du Nord. He was a good-natured giant with a yellow Gitane cigarette dangling eternally from the corner of his mouth. 'Poor little rich girl, alone on the beach, alone and so rich . . .' Time marches on, and people have since disappeared. Mama died first. Next, Clo-Clo electrocuted himself. Then my father's gentle cousin, whose business had gone downhill, gave up the ghost, leaving an inconsolable tribe of children and animals behind. My wardrobe is now full of button-down shirts, and I believe the small record shop now sells chocolates. Since the Berck train leaves from the Gare du Nord, perhaps one day I shall ask someone to check on their way through.

'Well done, Céleste!' cries Sylvie. 'Mama, I'm bored,' Théophile at once complains. It is 5 p.m. The chimes of the hospital clock, which usually strike me as cheerful, assume funereal tones as the time for farewells draws near. Wind begins to whip up the sand. The tide has gone out so far that swimmers are nothing but tiny dots on the horizon. The children run to stretch their legs on the beach once more before leaving, and Sylvie and I remain alone and silent, her hand squeezing my inert fingers. Behind dark glasses that reflect a flawless sky, she softly weeps over our shattered lives.

We return to my room for the final leavetaking. 'How do you feel, buddy?' asks Théophile. His buddy's throat is tight, his hands are sunburnt, and his **coccyx** hurts from

---

coccyx: bone at base of spine

sitting on it too long, but he has had a wonderful day. And what about you kids, what will you carry back from this field-trip into my endless solitude?

They have left. The car will already be speeding towards Paris. I sink into contemplation of a drawing brought by Céleste, which we immediately pinned to the wall: a kind of two-headed fish with blue-lashed eyes and multicoloured scales. It has the shape of the mathematical symbol for infinity. Sun streams in through the window. It is the hour when its rays fall straight upon my pillow. In the commotion of departure I forgot to signal for the curtains to be drawn. A nurse will be in before the world comes to an end.

Jean-Dominique Bauby died in March 1997.

Activities

Accident

1   Imagine you are the woman who finds the car after the accident. Describe to the police what you saw and what you did.

2   Make notes about the physical state of each member of the family after the accident: Rosemyn (who is telling the story), Mum, Dad and Phoebe. You will need to look back at pages 41–46.

3   The extract you have read gives you a good sense of the whole book, which is called *I must tell you something*.

   • Who would you recommend such a book to, and why?

   • Who might not like the book, and why not?

Knee-deep in glass

4   Zlata's diary is described as a true story of the war in Sarajevo. Pick out three details that make the events she describes real to you, and explain why you have chosen them.

5   Imagine that it is May 1992. Prepare a two-minute presentation to your school's charity committee to put the case for supporting the victims of the fighting in Sarajevo.

Through a glass darkly

6   List what you find out about the children, Théophile and Céleste, from the diary. In what ways are they different?

7   Explain what you would find most terrible about being Jean-Dominique, the father, if you were in his situation.

Overall

8 Write two or three entries for a diary covering an important time in your life.

Section 4
Animals

When you mention the word rabbit to most people they immediately go 'Ah'. Yet the same people are normally not so complimentary when you mention the words frog, toad, snake, octopus or squid. These extracts may help you to understand why this is the case.

Peta
John Crompton

At some point in our childhood many of us have come across a wounded wild animal. We try to help by putting the creature into a warm box and providing it with the right food. For most of us our efforts are in vain and the creature dies anyway. But this is another story . . .

As I rounded a country lane corner on my bike one day I almost ran over a baby rabbit. It crouched – tiny, dark brown, still – against the stony surface, and when I stopped and dropped my bike in the hedge, the rabbit remained rigid. But when I bent down to pick it up, it hopped away towards a gate into a field. The gate was meshed with wire netting and the little animal tried to run through the wire. I cornered it and picked it up. It was hardly more than a handful. It kicked at my hand with its back legs, its rounded, not yet properly grown, ears laid back down its neck.

I put the rabbit down the front of my shirt and cycled carefully home.

'Just in time for tea,' said my father as I entered the kitchen. 'Well, will you look at that now,' as I gently brought out my capture.

'It's very young, isn't it?' said my mother. 'Too young to leave its mother, surely?'

'I'm going to bring it up,' I announced. 'Can I have a hot-water bottle and some milk and honey, please?'

'You're not poorly, are you?' asked my mother. 'Oh, for the rabbit. Yes, of course.'

'I don't think anyone ever managed to bring up and keep a wild rabbit,' my father said. 'And you'll have to keep feeding it all night long, you know.'

I did know. But I was determined. I found a large cardboard box, put the warm hot-water bottle at the bottom, covered with a piece of clean rag, and put the rabbit on top. Then I made a milk and water and honey mixture and warmed it up.

My father washed out a dropper from an old eye medicine bottle, and I loaded it with the mixture and squeezed the liquid into the baby rabbit's mouth. The poor animal took four droppers-full straight off. Then I put some cabbage leaves in the box, closed the lid and put the whole thing in my bedroom.

Three times during the night I reheated the mixture and fed the rabbit. Towards dawn I found it had eaten some of the cabbage. What seemed only a few minutes of sleep later my father brought me a cup of tea in bed and I reported progress.

'Partly weaned, then,' he said. 'Able to take some solid food. Good thing it's holidays or you wouldn't be able to keep feeding it all day.'

I fell asleep again, but woke with a guilty start a couple of hours later and went down to the kitchen to heat up the feed.

'Try some oats and wheatgerm,' said my mother.

'Thanks,' I said. 'I'm starving.'

'Not for you. For the rabbit. Mix it up with the milk.'

The baby certainly liked that and it had also finished off the cabbage. I warmed up the hot-water bottle again. Then I had my own breakfast.

And so the routine went on, feed after feed, cabbage leaf after cabbage leaf. Till, after a fortnight, I began to reduce the liquid and to offer the oats dry, in a small bowl, with chopped carrot and grass. That seemed to be fine. She took well to the greenery and oats, and after a month I gave no more milk. At that point I built her a snug hutch and set it on top of the hutch belonging to my ordinary, tame rabbit, a big bruiser of a buck called Nicky. I had hopes of mating the wild one, now called Peta, with Nicky, when she was old enough.

Peta grew up quickly. She was never very big, fat and jolly like Nicky: she remained always shy, unwilling to be stroked or picked up. But she had grown up, and I really was keeping a wild rabbit. She was not keen on Nicky, however, cowering away from the bustling, bouncing buck when I put them together. He leapt upon her with careless brutality, and I could see she was not willing to accept him. The trouble was, I did not know enough about when to put them together, not learning till some years later that you have to wait until the doe is on heat and ready for the buck. So I respected Peta's shyness, feeling that even if I had brought her to adulthood she was not going to breed.

Three years I kept her, till the day my mother had been asked to give the rabbits their evening feed and she left Peta's cage door unlatched. We never saw her again.

King Kong and Fafnir
John Crompton

In this extract John Crompton spends some time researching exactly how high and how far frogs can really jump. He also goes on a snake-hunting expedition.

There were plenty of frogs in the long grass in our garden. A cunning way to catch them was to put down a plank or a big stone one day and come back the next. Likely at least one frog had taken advantage of this cool, sheltered place, for frogs must keep damp. It fascinated me that no two frogs were ever the same colour. They could be light, medium or dark green and every shade of brown from biscuit to nearly black. Occasional ones managed yellow or orange, and even reddish. All had big eyes, mounted in special pop-up blisters on the tops of their heads, and all had triangles of shiny, dark brown skin behind the eyes. Whenever I found one with a new or particularly striking colour, I would take it indoors to show my mother.

'Yes, very nice, dear,' she would say, backing away. 'But it looks so slimy. Do keep it away. Are you sure you have tight hold of it?'

'Well, of course frogs are a bit slippery,' I would say. 'But they are really rather charming, don't you think? And very good for eating slugs.'

They also vary in their ability to jump. Their large, powerful back legs are kept doubled under them, ready to be unleashed in a sudden spring. My friend William and I spent hours during one summer measuring how high and how far frogs could jump, and holding frog races.

Each frog was put down just behind a starting line and then touched on its back end by one of us while the other marked the exact spot where it landed. Each frog was given three jumps and the average distance calculated. It was harder to judge how high they went, though we had a piece of string stretched across the jumping-path at a height of two feet six inches, and any frog who cleared that had his next jump very carefully watched to try and judge how much he cleared it by.

The record for long jump was held by a medium-sized, rather thin frog, whom we called Nipper. Nipper was almost grey when first rounded up from under the decoy plank, though he turned khaki-coloured after a couple of days in the big glass tank I kept frogs in. Nipper jumped the amazing distance of seven feet seven and a half inches. That was on his first jump. William and I were so impressed that Nipper nearly got away as he made two further good leaps before we thought to chase him. After those he managed only six feet two on his second jump, and we decided to rest him a bit before setting him on his third attempt.

The previous record-holder, a fat, squat, muscular-looking frog called Blinder, was fetched to see what he could do. But he was out of form. Whereas his previous best had been six feet eight, he could now do only five feet nine. He was put away again in disgrace. And the fantastic Nipper, after his rest, sailed a cool eight feet six through the air. So his average was, on that occasion, seven feet five. On another day he put in one monster bound of eight feet eleven but he never broke his own record average.

'It's his strength-to-weight ratio,' said William. 'When he was first caught he was thin and mean and hungry. The best frog-jumper is a hungry frog-jumper, but he's been sitting in that tank with too many worms and slugs, and he's gone soft. He could do nine feet easily if he was pushed. But why should he? He has it cushy in there. I say let him go and find a better.'

So Nipper was released, along with Blinder, and we worked on the height record-holder, Slipstream, who we reckoned had cleared four feet. We tried to convert him to long jump but he never broke the seven-foot barrier, so he was let loose, too.

'Mind you,' said William, 'if you work out what a seven-foot jump is to an animal only nine inches or so long, it's pretty tremendous. It means he can jump nine times his own length. If I could do that I would be able to jump over fifty feet. And without a run, too.'

A few more measurements showed us that the smaller frogs could actually jump farther, compared to their own length, than the big fat ones. But the big ones were impressive with their sheer size. The daddy of them all was called King Kong. With his back legs stretched out behind him, he was over a foot long, and the top of his head was five inches above the ground.

'That surely is one hell of a frog,' said William. 'Let's weigh him.'

But my mother objected strongly to the use of her kitchen scales for that piece of research. 'I don't care if it's the biggest frog in the world. You are not putting that nasty, smelly thing on my scales. I make cakes with what is put on those. And take it out of my kitchen.'

Unfortunately, when my father asked to hold King Kong for a minute, the crafty monster made a jump for it, and it took three of us some chasing round the kitchen and hall to recapture him, during which the poor beast somehow managed to break a toe. So we thought it best to release him.

*

The tank was used next for newts, which are related to frogs. They are amphibians, too. That is, they can live on land and in water, though newts seem to like to spend most of their time in water. They look like small lizards, only with webbed feet and flat tails. Our newts did not do much except swim about a bit, so we took them back to the stream we had caught them in and turned our ambition to snakes.

Unwisely, I mentioned the snakes to my mother. 'Oh, John, you're not going to go near any snakes, are you?'

My father was soon summoned to prevent me. He said, 'Well, it's all right, you know, if you can tell the harmless ones from the poisonous one.'

'Isn't it best to be on the safe side and leave them all alone?'

But my father was all ready to give a little talk about British snakes.

'In this country we have three snakes: the adder, the smooth snake and the grass snake. The smooth snake is –'

'What about the viper?' my mother demanded.

'That's another name for the adder. As I was saying, the smooth snake is rare now, and I doubt if there are any round here. The adder or viper is usually light brown or grey in colour with a very definite zigzag pattern of black line down its back. It has a blunt tail and a rather triangular head. The grass snake, however, is greenish or greyish and has no line down the back. Furthermore, it has a very distinctive yellow mark behind each eye, on the back of its jaws. And a long tapering tail and a thinner head.'

He fetched out a book with pictures to show us. I had already seen a lot of grass snakes and had no doubts about being able to spot them. Despite my mother's pleadings, therefore, I refused to give up my plan of turning the glass tank into a snakery.

William and I set out every day for the area of streams and ditches by the river, because grass snakes like to swim, and live largely on frogs. We had a butterfly net, a large plastic bag and a forked stick. We knew that the main hazard in dealing with grass snakes was that they made a dreadful smell when frightened.

'Did you know grass snakes can grow eight feet long?' asked William. 'I think we should try and catch one at least five feet long if possible, even if it does let off a fearful pong.'

'Right!' I agreed firmly, but I was secretly daunted at the thought of eight feet of snake, however harmless.

On the third day we actually spotted a huge one. It was asleep, curled up on an old moorhen's nest in the middle of a sluggish stream. From ten feet away we could see that its thickest coil was at least three inches in diameter.

'We'll have to wade out for it,' William said quietly, in the tone of voice of someone expecting someone else to take action.

'Right!' I agreed, and began slowly to take off my shoes. 'Blast! It's escaping.'

Unhurriedly the snake began to pour itself into the water, coil by coil. When it had still not taken its last bit off the old nest, its head was at least six feet away. Then it dived and I do not think either of us much liked the idea of going into the stream and poking about under the water for the likes of that length of serpent.

We did see other snakes but all slid away into bushes, streams or holes before they could be apprehended with hands, net or stick. Eventually we did catch one, however. It was well away from cover, making its snaky way down the gutter of the road outside William's house. Seeing its pursuers, it put on a spurt to all of four miles an hour and was soon curling itself forlornly round my hand. It managed to squirt out a small amount of milky liquid, which smelled rather of flour and water and not very terrible. When we took the creature indoors to a ruler, it measured a massive ten inches long.

'It'll grow,' said William. 'Start in a small way, you know.'

'In ten years it might make it to two feet or so, you mean.'

'Look on the bright side,' he said. 'This one won't need too much food.'

The creature was called Fafnir and installed in the tank with sand, plants, worms, slugs and a bowl of water. It promptly buried itself in the sand and remained there most of the time.

We dug it out a couple of times a day. 'Must make it hand-tame,' said William. 'Then, when it's eight feet long, it will be used to us and friendly.'

In fact Fafnir was released in the autumn.

'Must let him hibernate,' said my father. 'Grass snakes hole up for the winter and only come out again with next spring's sun. And he has to choose his own spot.'

'Don't let him loose in the garden,' begged my mother. 'I don't want to find myself faced with that next time I go for some beans.'

Before the Second World War, my father used to watch a man who actually caught adders by picking them up quickly by the tails and slotting them neatly into milk-bottle-shaped containers before they knew quite what had happened. He was paid so much per snake, for the captives were sent to Germany to have their poison removed and used in a medicine for snakebite. Apparently the snakes across the English Channel have a more deadly bite than ours.

This swift and confident snake-catcher operated on the Isle of Wight, over an area particularly rich in adders. I have been there and observed them. There are dozens to be seen, sunning themselves on the rocks and bare hillsides above the sea near Blackgang. Big plump adders, bright and shiny-scaled, the zigzags down their backs standing out against the paler background, when you spot them, but helping to make them nearly invisible when they keep still.

The biggest I ever saw was nearly five feet long, I would guess. Big, for an adder. So impressive was the sight that, even though the magnificent, venom-carrying reptile was twenty feet away and not going to do me any harm, I picked up a large rock and threw it at those thick handsome coils. I was ashamed at once and half expected the angry biter to come for me, to punish my stupid spite with its outsize teeth – teeth that work like hypodermic needles, injecting the clear, oily poison into the punctures they make. As I ran away, suddenly frightened, I saw the beast dive under a bramble patch.

I have often wondered how there is enough food for all the adders in that spot. They eat frogs, lizards, mice, small birds – just about anything that moves, including, I suspect, smaller adders. Like all snakes they eat a lot and seldom. One frog or mouse will last even a big adder a month. It is surprising how a snake with a fairly small head can manage to swallow an animal wider than itself, as I discovered when I saw both an adder and a grass snake in the middle of swallowing prey.

The grass snake, a modest three-footer, was disposing of an unfortunate frog. The snake's jaws had become disconnected and the neck and body simply stretched to take the bulge, which travelled slowly down the length of the green body to about two-thirds of the way to the end of the tail. The adder I saw, a two-footer, was dealing with a small lizard, using the same technique: the jaws spread apart and the swelling of the food just travelled down the body.

In the case of the grass snake, William had to go and pick it up, of course. He wanted to know how much fatter the snake was after its meal. The snake promptly set about the rather difficult business of sicking the frog up again. William put the poor snake down but it was determined to be rid of the frog, which came out looking somewhat thin and crushed, before heading off.

'It didn't have to do that,' said William. 'I haven't any use for a spewed-up frog. It's wasted its breakfast, dinner and tea for weeks doing that.'

I noticed he did not interfere with the adder when the lizard had been consumed.

Giant snakes
Simon Welfare and John Fairley

Are you the type of person who goes to the zoo or safari park but quietly avoids the snake-house? Or are you the person clamouring to be the first to hold the snake in a wildlife talk? Whether we love them or hate them, most of us would admit that stories about snakes fascinate us. In this extract you can find out the truth about how big these snakes really get.

In September 1990, a photograph arrived in Europe which gave a chilling new impetus to the controversy about the size and gruesome appetites of giant snakes.

In the picture, an enormous anaconda lay dead, dumped in the back of a truck. Comparing it with the spectators clustered round the side, it is easy to believe that the snake measured the thirty-five feet that its captors claimed.

But the eye is not riveted so much by the length of the snake, but more by the huge and distended lump in the snake's middle. For inside this grotesque protuberance is the body of a full-grown man – a Brazilian Indian fisherman.

His comrades had watched helplessly as he was ensnared while he stood in the water and then slowly eaten from the head downward. It took ten minutes or more for the snake to consume him.

A witness said: 'One of his feet was still hanging out and you could hear his bones crunching.' The snake was eventually shot and the body recovered.

There have been many stories of humans eaten by snakes – an eight-year-old boy eaten by a python in

Burma in 1972, a fourteen-year-old shepherd boy, Johannes Mokau, killed by a python near Johannesburg in 1972, as well as cows, horses, and – as in *The Swiss Family Robinson* – donkeys.

But how big can snakes grow? The French explorer Serge Bonacase claimed to have killed a snake of seventy-five feet in the Araguaya area of Brazil, and a French priest travelling up the Amazon reckoned one anaconda at above eighty feet.

Colonel Fawcett, the British explorer, measured a snake he shot on the River Negro at sixty-two feet.

Yet no snake in captivity has reliably been measured beyond the twenty-seven feet which a python called Cassius attained at Knaresborough Zoo in Yorkshire in England.

There are skins preserved which suggest lengths of up to thirty-five feet. But no one has yet claimed the 15,000 dollars on offer from the Bronx Zoo in New York for a snake exceeding thirty feet.

Snake skins can be stretched spectacularly when removed from their owner's skeleton, and may account for some of the large claims in museums. Intrepid travellers are hardly keen to transport bulky evidence through remote jungles.

But the evidence of, now, quite a number of photographs would suggest that snakes far bigger than any specimens that have reached the zoologists of Europe or America do indeed still lurk in the forests and jungles of the earth.

Nature's nightmare
Ronald N Rood

People usually think of whales and sharks when they think about the monsters of the deep. This extract shows that the squid should be as respected and feared as any other sea creature.

They have reached out and torn sailors from life rafts. They have reduced a huge tuna to head and bones before the hooked fish could be landed. Large members of the clan even dare to battle with the sperm whale. Yet most people who know anything about the squid – one of the sea's most bizarre and terrifying creatures – assume it is some sort of octopus, because it has snaky arms at the end of a bullet-shaped body. This is like comparing a tiger with an alley cat.

A 50 lb octopus with a 10 ft arm spread is a giant; the biggest squid are ten times as large. Octopuses retreat singly into scattered holes on the ocean bottom; though one may occasionally maul a diver who surprises it in its den, most leave the scene when man appears. Squid, on the other hand, may attack anything – even anchors, boat hooks or the hull of a ship. They work in ravenous mobs in open water. An attack by one may be the signal for a frenzied rush by others.

Like the octopus, the squid has eight arms with rows of suckers – but with the added touch of tooth-like horny rings around the edge of each sucker; and there are two more arms, called tentacles, which have no equal in all Nature. Like long rubber cables, they can stretch far beyond the reach of the other arms or snap back until they are nearly hidden. Armed at the tip with suckers (some 20 ft specimens even have retractile claws), the tentacles shoot out towards a victim, clamp fast and pull the prey back into the squid's writhing nest of arms with the parrot-like beak in the centre.

Unlike the baggy octopus, a squid is long and thin, with two horizontal fins at one end. It travels by jet propulsion. Taking in water by opening the muscular mantle that surrounds its body like a loose overcoat, the squid squirts it out through a powerful siphon near the head. This shoots the squid backwards, slender rear section first. Rocketing through the water, it can overtake nearly anything that swims. By reversing the flexible siphon, it shuttles back and forth through a school of fish. The two tentacles whip out like living lassos, catching fish after fish – killing far beyond its needs. Just a bite out of each one, and then it is dropped for a new victim.

When I saw my first living squid in an aquarium, I had the uncanny feeling that I was being watched. The eyes are intelligent, alert, arrestingly human. Each eye has a movable lens to focus on objects at any distance, a refinement that is possessed by no other invertebrates outside the class. It has an iris and a pupil, just as the human eye has. Sometimes there are even eyelids.

This would not be so surprising if the squid were close to us on the family tree of evolution. But squid are molluscs, with a history that stretches back 400 million years, far beyond that of man. As the ages passed, their ancestors – some with dozens of arms – developed shells like ice-cream cones, sometimes 12 ft long. Larger types had coiled shells, like a ram's horn. Today they have no outer shells but are built around a cartilaginous internal rod called the 'pen'. It is the internal support of the cuttlefish – a member of the same class as the squid, and closely resembling it – which provides the cuttlebone that is often given to budgerigars.

The numbers of squid are fantastic. Ships sometimes get false bottom readings from echo sounders owing, some scientists say, to millions of squid suspended halfway to the bottom, feeding on plankton. Sometimes this layer is found on the surface. One ship sailed for two hours through a solid sea of squid stretching to the horizon in all directions.

The squid is a living kaleidoscope. Rob it of its prey, and it flashes an angry red. Frighten it, and it turns a pale, watery colour. It can be mottled like the sand or rippled like the surface. It has thousands of tiny colour cells, opening and closing like draw-string bags. One instant they are open, showing their coloured lining; a fifth of a second later they close. Deep-water squid may have hundreds of light-producing areas, sparkling like fireflies.

If camouflage does not work against a predatory enemy, the squid has an emergency measure – it shoots out a blob of black, gooey 'ink' through the siphon to form a smoke-screen. Squid from the depths even have luminous ink to make a flare in the water while the darkened owner sneaks away.

Only rarely does a really giant squid come up from the depths to be seen by man. An occasional specimen is vomited up by a dying sperm whale; and fishermen sometimes see an injured one floating on the surface.

On March 25, 1941, the troopship *Britannia* was sunk in mid-Atlantic. A dozen men clung to a tiny raft. Only one or two could sit on it at a time, while the rest waited their turn in the water. Suddenly one of them cried out. Horrified, the others saw a great squid throw a tentacle around his body. Then the other tentacle clamped fast. Before their eyes, the unspeakable creature broke the sailor's hold on the raft and pulled him to his death.

Soon afterwards, another man felt a tentacle grasp his leg. For some reason, it let go again. But where the suckers had fastened, they left raw, bleeding sores. The scars, like the prints of bottle caps, were still visible two years later.

On October 26, 1873, near Portugal Cove, Newfoundland, two men and a boy were out fishing when they spotted a floating mass in the water. It hung limply, like a piece of wreckage. But, prodded with a **gaff**, it came to life, reared up and lunged at their boat. Its arms spread out, exposing a beak in the centre twice as big as a man's head.

It slipped one tentacle across the gunwale like a python, pulling the little craft towards that hideous mouth. It gouged at the planking, staring at the men with dinner-plate eyes. Then it threw an arm over the boat to secure its hold and sank beneath the water. Spellbound, the men watched their boat tip until water rushed in over the side.

Twelve-year-old Tom Piccot saved them all. He grabbed a hatchet and began to chop at the grisly creature. Not until he had hacked it free did it drop away. Then it lay alongside the boat and glared at them, its great cylindrical body pulsating and throwing out clouds of ink.

They raced for the shore. Their countrymen would not believe their tale until they showed the evidence – a 19ft tentacle like a heavy rope, lying in the bottom of their boat. Beside it was another chunk, as big as a man's arm.

The longest squid actually measured was 57 ft, found on a New Zealand beach in 1888. No one knows how large squid may grow. Several authorities think they may reach 70 ft, including 50 ft tentacles. Such a creature would weigh well over a ton. There is an interesting point for further speculation, too. The suckers of a 50 ft squid leave circular rings on the skin of the sperm whale about

---

gaff: pole tipped with a metal hook, used for landing fish

4 in. across. Yet whales have been found with round scars 18 in. across – more than four times greater than scars made by the largest squid known.

Compared with such giants, most squid are tiny – less than 8 in. long. These constitute one of the most important food items in the ocean. Schools of fish cut great swaths through their millions. (It is this fact, plus their own cannibalism, which keeps them from overrunning the ocean completely.) Porpoises and killer whales often gorge on them. Man has long enjoyed them, too – consuming half a million tons a year.

The mating procedure of the squid is extraordinary. Sometimes the male 'courts' the female, or fights with other males for her favour. At other times he merely seizes her abruptly in a many-armed embrace. Then, since he is a cannibal, he may forget himself. Many a squid romance ends as abruptly as it starts – with a squid dinner.

The sex organs of both male and female are hidden deep within the cavity of the mantle. The male squid's sperm are wrapped in small packets called spermatophores. With one of his arms he reaches into his mantle cavity, takes a few packets from the genital organ and places them in the mantle cavity of the female. The wrapping unravels, releasing the sperm. Later, as the eggs pass through the female on their way to the outside, they are fertilised by the waiting sperm.

The female gently blows the fertilised eggs out through the siphon and catches them in her arms. The eggs – from a few hundred to 30,000, depending on the species – are about the size of cooked tapioca. She presses them against underwater objects in foot-long, sticky strings, then swims away. The babies hatch in about a month. They are fierce little beauties with rainbow colours, looking like exquisite rice-grain editions of their parents.

They spread quickly, but not before fish scoop them up in great numbers. So the chain of life continues.

Today, the squid has taken on scientific importance in the study of nerves and mental health. Biologists have discovered a giant nerve in several species that is 40 times thicker than the largest nerve worked on previously. Instead of working with fibres thinner than a human hair, scientists can now use one that approaches the diameter of a wooden match. Since nerve tissue is much the same no matter what animal it comes from, this should facilitate research in nerve action, vital body activities and hormones.

In this way, scientists probe into twentieth-century health and disease, aided by a terrifying creature whose beginnings can be traced back almost as far as any living animal on earth today.

Activities

Peta

1   Write a 10-point guide to rearing a baby rabbit. Make your instructions clear and concise. You may wish to illustrate your guide to ensure that the information stands out.

King Kong and Fafnir *and* Giant snakes

2   Imagine that you are writing a book about snakes. You decide to include a page on snakes of Britain and a page on grisly facts about snakes: prepare the pages.

You may wish to set out your pages so that the information is clear to see and to illustrate them to make them attractive to look at.

Nature's nightmare

3   Divide your page in half like this:

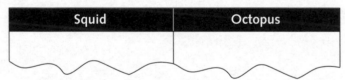

Squid	Octopus

Under each heading write down what you learn about the creature from the extract.

4   What evidence is there in this article to prove that huge specimens of giant squid exist?

5   How is the squid useful to man today?

Overall

6   Create an information book spread (two adjoining pages) for an animal you have invented. It can be large or small, wild or tame. The book is aimed at the 9–12 age group.

Section 5
UFOs: fact or fantasy?

Unidentified flying objects have been with us for a long time. Modern-day interest in such things is often dated from Kenneth Arnold's sighting of a 'flying saucer' in June 1947. Actually, he never called it a flying saucer but that is how it came to be known. Here are two reports of the incident. As you'll discover, even the accounts do not agree exactly about what happened.

Report Number One
Marc Gascoigne

This report comes from the opening of a book which considers many of the modern UFO 'sightings' and attempts to distinguish those which are genuine mysteries from those which probably have a logical explanation.

On that day in 1947, Kenneth Arnold was flying home in his single-engine plane over the Cascade Mountains in Washington State, USA. He was 32, a businessman and an experienced pilot, so it was no surprise that he decided to take a small diversion to see if he could spot a wrecked Marine Corps C-46 transport plane which had crashed recently.

As he banked over the small town of Mineral, about 40 kilometres from Mount Rainier, he was dazzled by a bright, blue-white flash. At first he thought it must have been a reflection off another plane, perhaps an Air Force Mustang buzzing him. As he looked around, he saw another flash and then, to the north and left of him, a most amazing sight: nine silvery, crescent-shaped discs were flying in a long line. The objects were following the contours of the mountains, and every so often one or another would dip slightly, causing the Sun to flash off it. Comparing their course with the landscape, he estimated that they were strung out over perhaps eight kilometres, and appeared to be travelling at around 1900 kilometres per hour! The strange craft crossed his path and he could clearly see that they had no tails. As they flew, they continued to bob and weave; later he said they were like 'speedboats in rough water'. It was obvious that they were something strange. They flew off, out of sight, and a troubled Arnold made for Yakima Air Base.

At first, he told the flight controllers when he landed, they might have been a secret type of aircraft, which he hoped was American rather than Russian. A fellow pilot suggested that they were guided missiles from the nearby Moses Lake testing range – but crescent-shaped? Eventually Arnold set off for his destination, Pendleton, Oregon. When he got there, he found that the controllers at Yakima had mentioned his strange sighting and word had got out: reporters were waiting, and Arnold gladly told them his story.

Next morning, the Seattle *Post-Intelligencer* bore the headline 'MYSTERY DISKS HURTLING ACROSS THE SKY'. The story was picked up and was soon being beamed to newspapers around the world. There was much debate across America. Most analysts were respectful: Arnold, although an experienced pilot, must have been mistaken in what he saw; he witnessed a mirage or an optical illusion. As the story spread, and a proper explanation still couldn't be found, the pilot was dismissed as a crackpot and a hoaxer. Arnold eventually admitted that he wished he'd kept the story to himself.

If he had, that wouldn't have been an end to the matter. There were eight other sightings in the same State that day, and twenty more over the next few days. UFO fever began to spread across America. By the end of 1947, over 850 sightings had been publicized, and the Air Force was forced to institute Project Sign to collect and examine all such reports.

Report Number Two
Brian Ball

The writer of the book from which this report is taken is particularly interested in showing how we started to think about flying saucers. Here is the explanation he gives.

How did UFOs come to be called *flying saucers*?

To answer that question we have to go back to June 1947, when an American civilian pilot called Kenneth Arnold joined in the search for a missing aircraft. All pilots in the area had been requested to watch out for the wreckage of a Marine Transport plane thought to have come down in the mountains. The sky was clear and visibility was excellent. At two o'clock in the afternoon, Mr Arnold was flying at around nine thousand feet near Mount Rainier in the Rocky Mountains when below him he saw a flash of bright light.

And then a whole series of bright lights.

There were nine of them, flying in and out of the peaks with a dipping, zig-zagging movement. Their size was about fifty feet across – about the length and width of a 1940s medium-sized aircraft. But they didn't look like any plane Mr Arnold had seen.

They looked like saucers.

'They looked like *what*?' a reporter asked him later, when he was interviewed about the mysterious discs.

So Mr Arnold explained that he had seen nine silvery disc-shaped objects flying in formation below him, and that they seemed to be skipping along in the kind of flight you would expect if you skimmed a round flat stone on water. They were moving faster than any aircraft he had ever seen, and they had the shape of saucers.

The newsmen were fascinated. They wanted to know if the strange objects had wings.

'No,' said Mr Arnold. 'No wings.'

But how did the silvery discs manage to fly? the news reporters asked. What kind of engines powered them?

'I don't know,' said Mr Arnold.

Mr Arnold hadn't seen any engines. The objects were discs, not at all the usual shape of an aircraft – and there were no wings, no tailplane, no engines.

'So they weren't aircraft?'

'I don't know what they were,' said Mr Arnold.

'And there were nine of them?'

'Yes, nine.'

'Nine shining lights. You really saw them, sir?'

So Mr Arnold went over it all again. He had seen a flash of light first, then the discs skipping along like saucers.

'Like saucers flying?' said one newsman. 'Is that what you saw?'

'Like flying saucers?' said another news reporter. '*Flying saucers!*'

The Roswell incident
Rowan Wilson

Another even stranger happening also took place in 1947, about a month later. The incident centred on a town called Roswell in New Mexico, and the alleged cover-up of what happened is as mysterious as the episode itself. The whole series of events was unusual from start to finish . . .

William 'Mac' Brazel worked on the Foster Ranch, north of Roswell. On the night of July 4, he heard a tremendous crash come from out in the fields. It was strange, unlike the thunder that had been rumbling dully through most of the evening. Brazel decided to keep his eyes peeled out when he rode to the ranch the next morning.

What he found was torn metal sheeting and large chunks of debris, which covered a field south of the ranch. All around, the light shiny foil fluttered and glinted in the breeze. The wreckage centred on an arroyo or small cliff and spread across acres of desert scrub. The early morning sun made the whole field shine. Brazel picked up some of the foil. It was indeed as light as it looked. However, when crumpled into a ball, it resolutely unfolded and smoothed itself out. Investigating further, Brazel found that there were many small beams or rods strewn across the field. These were thin and as light as **dowling**, yet too rigid to break. Try as he might, Brazel could only bend them slightly. When the pressure was

---

dowling: narrow wooden or metal rods used to join two surfaces by fitting into matching holes in each

released they sprang right back. Intrigued, Brazel tried his knife on the debris – it would not cut. Burning with matches did not even mark it.

Brazel had company that morning – William Proctor, the young son of a neighboring family. The two agreed that they should take some of the material over to the Proctors to get another opinion.

Loretta and Floyd Proctor examined the foil with interest. Floyd tried to cut and burn it (just like Brazel had), with the same lack of success. Brazel suggested that the Proctors drive over and see the field, but they declined – they were too busy. It was a decision they would later regret.

Brazel returned home wondering what to do. The debris was in his way. But he decided to put off the decision until the weekend. He took Sunday afternoon off and drove in to see the Sheriff of Chaves County, George Wilcox, at his office in Roswell.

Covered in dust and wearing scruffy work clothes, Brazel was first seen by a deputy. The rancher explained his problem and brought out a piece of the foil-like debris to show what he was talking about. The deputy had never seen anything like it before. But since it had fallen from the sky, he suggested that it was military business.

Roswell, New Mexico, is surrounded by military bases. The closest was the Roswell Army Air Field, home of Bomber Squadron 509, the nuclear bomb wing. Also close by was the army listening post at Alamogordo. Finally, in the desert to the west of Roswell lay White Sands Testing Grounds, the home of US experimental aeronautics. After World War II, the creator of the V2 rocket bomb, Werner von Braun, had been brought to the US to work on secret weapon systems and the newly launched space program. His laboratory was also at White Sands.

At Roswell Army Air Field, Major Jesse A. Marcel was eating lunch when he took the phone call from Sheriff Wilcox. Marcel was the base's Intelligence Officer, which meant that the unidentified debris strewn across the Foster ranch fell within his jurisdiction.

He was intrigued by the description of the wreckage. So, taking a counterintelligence sergeant called Sheridan Cavitt with him, Marcel lost no time in leaving for Roswell. By the time that he arrived it was late afternoon, too late to drive out to the isolated debris field before dark. So Marcel and Cavitt accompanied Brazel back to the Foster ranch house and, as night fell, they examined a large piece of the wreckage that Brazel had dragged back from the field.

It was like nothing Marcel had ever seen. But at least a Geiger counter showed it was not radioactive. Several years earlier, New Mexico had been the site of some of the first nuclear weapons tests.

Early the next morning, Cavitt and Marcel made their way with Brazel out to the crash site. Examining more of the wreckage failed to bring any further enlightenment. Marcel was familiar with most kinds of military hardware, but looking at torn silver shreds clinging to the arroyo, he could not see anything akin to any weapon, rocket or balloon. It was very disturbing.

The metallic beams in the field had a cross section less than a half inch square and were as light as aluminium – yet so strong that, exerting all his strength, Marcel could only bend them slightly. And when he released the pressure, they straightened out immediately. Studying one of the beams closely, he could just make out lines of markings in two colors, like Chinese script. The phrase that kept crossing Marcel's mind was 'flying saucer.' The local and national news were full of sightings. And here, out in the desert, was mysterious wreckage that defied categorization. Hurriedly, Marcel gathered armfuls of the debris and loaded up his jeep.

Instead of taking it back to Roswell Air Field, Marcel brought it to his home. He wanted his family to see it. Jesse Jr remembers that morning well. He and his mother were still in bed when Marcel arrived. He quickly roused them and told them to help him carry the pieces in from the car. They spread the wreckage out on the kitchen floor and began trying to fit it together.

Marcel's wife, Viaud, noticed the strange markings on the beams and pointed them out to Jesse Jr. He later explained that they were leaves, circles and other simple figures. Finally, Marcel packaged up the debris and took it back to the base.

It was the following morning before Colonel William Blanchard, the base CO, examined Marcel's find. He ordered Marcel to take the debris to Fort Worth Army Air Field and show it to General Ramey. About noon that day, Tuesday, July 8, 1947, First Lieutenant Walter Haut (Information Officer for Roswell Army Air Field) composed a press release about Brazel's discovery and distributed it to the local radio stations and newspapers. The afternoon papers received it in time for that day's editions. The *Daily Illni* reported it under the headline 'A.P. Wire Burns With "Captured Disk" Story.' The misprints in the article indicate that it had been typeset in a hurry. It read, 'Roswell N.M. The army air forces here today announced a flying disc [*sic*] had been found on a ranch near Roswell and is in army possession.

'The Intelligence office reports that it gained possession of the "Dis:" [*sic*] through the cooperation of a Roswell rancher and Sheriff George Wilson [*sic*] of Roswell.

CO: Commanding Officer

'The disc landed on a ranch near Roswell sometime last week. Not having phone facilities, the rancher, whose name has not yet been obtained, stored the disc until such time as he was able to contact the Roswell sheriff's office . . .

'. . . Residents near the ranch on which the disc was found reported seeing a strange blue light several days ago about three o'clock in the morning.'

The next morning, most of America was reading about the captured 'disc' over breakfast.

Whether all the debris was flown to Fort Worth, or just the part that Marcel recovered, is not known. Sergeant Robert Porter, who flew the B-29 that transported it, later reported that there were four boxes, the largest of which was three feet across and triangular.

Ramey received Marcel in his office, where the debris was already stacked in its boxes. Ramey had been fielding calls from newsmen ever since the Roswell press release and the entire situation was beginning to worry him. After a discussion with Marcel, Ramey decided on a press conference, during which the wreckage would be displayed to the media.

A few hours later, as the assembled journalists contemplated fragments of what was quite obviously a weather balloon, Warrant Officer Irving Newton (a weather officer), assured them – unnecessarily – that the wreckage on the floor of Ramey's office definitely originated on planet Earth. Marcel was present at the conference but kept his silence.

The weather balloon story was to remain the accepted view for many years – in fact until 1979, when Major Marcel decided to tell his own version of events at Fort Worth to journalist Bob Pratt.

According to Marcel, what happened was a simple switch. When he had arrived in the General's office that day, Ramey had insisted upon being shown the exact location of the crash site on some charts in another room. By the time they returned to the office, the wreckage that he had carefully ferried all the way from New Mexico had vanished, and in its place, laid out on brown paper, was a torn weather balloon. When Marcel had picked up some of the balloon to examine it, photos had been taken by the base's information officer. Ramey told Marcel that he would attend the press conference and would play along and keep his mouth shut.

Directly after the conference, Marcel said that Ramey had ordered him back to Roswell. Since it was clear that the army had launched a disinformation campaign, Marcel ordered his family to keep quiet about what they had seen that July morning.

Back at Roswell Army Air Field, Marcel found Sergeant Cavitt who had accompanied him on the first visit out to the Foster ranch. He asked him if he had prepared a report. Cavitt said that he had but could not show it to Marcel, since it was confidential. He added that the order came direct from Washington.

Marcel's first response was irritation since he outranked Cavitt. Eventually, he saw that the Army had the entire situation sewn up. They had used him as a **patsy**. He was not happy about it – but the opportunity to tell the truth had to wait for 30 years until journalist Bob Pratt came to interview him.

The year following the Pratt interview, Marcel appeared in a TV documentary called 'In Search Of,' which covered UFO conspiracy theories and alleged crashes. In the film, Marcel repeated his assertion that the debris he had recovered in 1947 was not the remains of a weather balloon, as shown in the official photos. As a result of this

---

patsy: fall-guy, someone easy to deceive or cheat

new exposure, interest in the Roswell incident flared up again. And as UFO investigators converged on the town and began asking questions, interesting facts began to emerge.

Most of the people who had been living in Roswell at the time of the crash were still around and they, like Marcel, had stories to tell about the days following the discovery on the Foster ranch.

William Woody, the young boy who had seen a slow shooting star on the night of the crash, told how he and his father had decided to go and look for the object they had seen. Early on the morning of July 5, 1947, they had climbed into their pickup truck and driven north on Route 285. As they approached the area where they guessed that the object had landed, they found that every exit east and west off the highway was blocked by military sentries.

Glen Dennis, the proprietor of Ballard Funeral Home in Roswell, told investigators that on the day after the crash, he had received phone calls from the Army Air Field's mortuary officer. The military wanted childsized coffins. Then the officer wanted to know if the coffins he had could be closed to form an airtight seal. As if this was not strange enough, the officer rang back 40 minutes later, to ask about embalming and the effects of embalming fluid on the blood and tissues of a corpse. He seemed to be eager to discover if preserving a body would make it impossible to carry out an accurate medical examination at a later date. Dennis told him that it would and the officer rang off.

Later that day, Dennis told investigators, he had driven out to the Air Field. Ballard's Funeral Home had the army contract to ferry wounded service personnel back to the base and that afternoon, a soldier (who had suffered some minor head injuries) needed Dennis's ambulance service. As they arrived at the base, Dennis saw three army ambulances parked outside the infirmary. Inside two of them, there were torn pieces of metal-like aeroplane wreckage. The third was closed and guarded by a Military Policeman.

As the contracted ambulance driver, Dennis had the run of the hospital's staff areas. Feeling thirsty, he decided to go in for a soft drink. Once inside, he detected that there was something wrong. People were rushing about and shouting. Dennis assumed that there had been a plane crash. A nurse stopped him as he entered the lounge. She was incredulous that he had got into the unit and told him to get out as fast as he could or there would be trouble.

While Dennis tried to explain that he had a right to be there, an officer noticed them and angrily ordered two Military Policemen to escort him out. The officer had heard Dennis mention the crash and before having him ejected, he made a stark threat – 'Don't tell anybody you saw anything. Somebody'll be picking your bones out of the sand.'

A couple of days later, Dennis contacted the nurse he had met that day and arranged a meeting at the officers' club. When she arrived, she was looking badly shaken, pale and nervous. She told him that the torn pieces of metal he had seen were not from a normal aeroplane. They were sections of a crashed spacecraft. The staff at the hospital had been treating the injured occupants of the craft when Dennis arrived.

On her prescription pad, the nurse drew a picture of one of these 'foreign bodies' as she called them. The bodies were humanoid, yet smaller than an average person and slight in build. The only exception to this was the head, which was bulbous and hairless. The creatures had facial features similar to humans. Their mouths were lipless and small, their nose was indented and they had no ears. Their bones, she said, were flexible and tough, like cartilage.

The nurse told Dennis that she had been told to take notes while doctors carried out an autopsy on three of the dead creatures. Two of the bodies were badly mutilated, while one seemed to have survived the crash and only died of exposure once on the ground. The damage to the corpses was such that the doctors suspected that they had been mauled by desert predators. Throughout the examination, an ammonia-like choking smell came from the aliens. Eventually, the autopsies had to be abandoned due to nausea and faintness caused by the gas. The bodies were bagged up and sent down to the morgue.

Dennis's story was precise and detailed. And, of course, quite incredible. Yet many people in Roswell were telling stories that seemed to support it. Frankie Rowe was the daughter of one of Roswell's fire fighters, Dan Dwyer. On July 5, 1947, Frankie remembered, her father had been called out early in the morning. Dwyer told his daughter that they had gone out about 30 miles northwest of Roswell into the desert and there seen 'a flying craft' crashed and wrenched to pieces. He said that it looked as if the main pieces of wreckage had already been cleared away before they got there. Dwyer also said that there were bodies at the crash site. Two were dead and bagged when they arrived, but one was alive and seemingly uninjured and capable of walking.

Later, Frankie said, the military had arrived and told them to keep quiet about what they knew of the crash. They had specifically told her, a ten-year-old girl at the time, that if she talked about what she had heard she was liable to get lost in the desert and never come back.

Activities

Report Number One

1   Make a list of what you learn about the 'flying saucers' from this report.

2   Do you think Arnold makes a good witness? Why, or why not?

Report Number Two

3   Make a list of what you learn about the 'flying saucers' from this second report.

Report Number One *and* Report Number Two

4   What differences can you see between the two reports?

5   What do you think is the purpose of the reports? Which report do you think is more useful, and why?

The Roswell incident

6   Write a letter that Mac Brazel might have sent to a friend to tell him the truth about what he found.

7   'Cover-up exposed.' Produce a magazine article in which you expose what you argue is a military cover-up of an alien crash-landing at Roswell. Aim your writing at the casual reader who will not want all the details but needs to be kept interested.

Overall

8   Design an information poster for a UFO Society that wants people to accept the idea of alien spacecraft and life forms.

Get Real!

9 Prepare notes for a one-minute case either *for* or *against* a belief in aliens. Use information from this section. You may also search out information from other sources.

Section 6
Crime

Throughout time there have been people who want to get rich quickly and think that the only way to do it is by taking something that does not belong to them. In these extracts you can find out what happened to a number of them.

A little stabbing
Terry Deary and Neil Tonge

Christopher Marlowe was a famous playwright of the sixteenth century. He lived at the same time as William Shakespeare but died young in a pub brawl. No one will ever really know what happened, but here is one version.

Date: Wednesday 30 May 1593
Place: Eleanor Bull's Tavern, Deptford, London

Mrs Bull mopped at the spilt ale on the table with a dirty cloth. It dribbled onto the sawdust on the floor. Suddenly, three men clattered down the stairs and fell into the room. Three of the men she'd let the upstairs room to.

'Mrs Bull! Oh, Mrs Bull!' the skinny Ingram Frizer gasped as he clutched at his head.

'What's wrong?' the woman snapped. Frizer was a well-known trickster who'd tried to cheat her more than once.

The man took his hand away from his head. It was soaked in blood. 'Murder!' he said hoarsely.

'Sit down,' she said briskly. Frizer's two friends, Skeres and Poley, helped him to a bench. The woman mopped at the head wounds with her ale cloth and sniffed. 'Not murder, Mr Frizer, just a couple of two-inch cuts. You'll not die. Who did it?'

'Marlowe,' the man moaned, 'Christopher Marlowe.'

The woman looked at the stairs and snatched a bread knife from the bar. 'Roaming around stabbing people, is he?'

The wounded man shook his head slowly. 'Not any more, he's not.

Mrs Bull relaxed. 'You overpowered him, then?'

Frizer's voice dropped to a whisper. 'I killed him!'

The landlady grabbed the man by the collar and marched him towards the stairs. 'Let's have a look at poor Mr Marlowe, shall we?' she demanded. Frizer couldn't argue. Skeres and Poley lurked behind as she threw open the door.

The body lay on the floor. One lifeless eye stared at the ceiling. The other was covered in blood from a neat wound just above it.

'I knew you were trouble, you three,' the woman moaned. 'That Mr Marlowe seemed such a nice young man. What happened?' She looked closely at the body and shook her head. 'Doesn't look a bad enough wound to kill a man that quick,' she muttered.

Frizer swayed and let himself fall onto the bed.

'He was lying here, on this bed. We had our backs to him, didn't we Poley?'

Poley nodded. The local men said Poley made his money from spying. 'Our backs to him,' he said.

'Suddenly he jumped up from the bed, snatched my dagger and started stabbing at my head!' Frizer groaned.

'I had Skeres on one side of me and Poley on the other. I couldn't get out of the way, could I?'

'He couldn't!' Skeres agreed. Everybody knew that Skeres was a cutpurse and a robber.

'If he attacked you from behind he could have killed you easily, not just scratched your scalp, Mr Frizer,' the landlady argued.

'I moved,' the man said lamely.

'Then he stabbed himself in the eye, did he?' Mrs Bull asked with a sneer.

'No!' Poley cried. 'I managed to get the dagger from him. We struggled. It went into his eye by accident.'

'A strange sort of accident. Doesn't look the sort of wound you'd get from a scuffle. Looks more like he was lying on his back when the knife went in,' the woman said carefully.

The three men looked at each other nervously.

'Just one of those things,' Poley mumbled.

'So what were you arguing about?' the landlady asked. 'I didn't hear any argument.'

'About the bill,' Frizer said quickly.

'And why didn't your two friends help?' she asked suspiciously.

'It wasn't our argument,' Skeres shrugged.

'You'll hang for this, Mr Frizer,' Mrs Bull said contentedly.

Frizer looked up slowly from the bed. A curious smile came over his face. 'Oh no I won't, Mrs Bull. Oh, no I won't.'

And he didn't.

A strange sort of accident indeed. But the jury decided that was just what it was. You might have decided the same if you'd been on the jury. But looking back over 400 years you have a few more facts to go on. Here they are . . .

The powerful and important Sir Thomas Walsingham was a friend of all of the men and could have helped them get away with a plan such as this. Christopher Marlowe was certainly his closest friend.

Marlowe was in deep trouble at the time of his 'death'. His friend, Thomas Kyd, had just been arrested for having writings which said that Jesus was not the Son of God. The punishment for this was death. Kyd said the writings belonged to Christopher Marlowe! (It did Kyd no good – he died after being 'put to torture' in prison a year later.)

Frizer went back to work for Walsingham after he had been tried for the murder of Marlowe.

So what happened in Mrs Bull's tavern that day? If you don't believe Frizer's story, here are two other stories that fit the facts . . .

The execution theory

Marlowe had been careless. He'd left those writings in Kyd's room. Marlowe would be arrested and executed. Marlowe was as good as dead.

Kyd had accused Marlowe. But if Marlowe went to court he might have brought Sir Thomas Walsingham into all this. That would never have done.

Sir Thomas called his three loyal cut-throats to him. He gave them their orders, 'Kill Marlowe and I will reward you well. Make it look like an accident and I'll use all my power to make sure the court lets you go free.'

The three agreed to meet Marlowe in the tavern. As the playwright lay drunk on the bed, Skeres and Poley held him down while Frizer pushed the knife into his eye. Skeres or Poley then gave Frizer a couple of cuts on the head to back up their story of a fight.

Or . . .

The escape theory

Sir Thomas Walsingham was a great friend of Christopher Marlowe. He heard that Marlowe was about to be arrested for a crime that could lead to his execution. Sir Thomas wanted to protect his friend.

He called the four men to his house and told them of his plan. Marlowe must leave the country as soon as possible. As soon as he was safe abroad the other three must take a stranger to Mrs Bull's tavern and kill him.

After the murder, Frizer must confess. Say it was a fight and that 'Marlowe' had been killed. When a man owns up to murder, the constables are interested in establishing the *killer* – not the identity of the *victim*. The stranger was buried in a grave named 'Christopher Marlowe' and the real Marlowe was safe.

Of course, the real Marlowe was a successful playwright. Imagine Marlowe wants to go on writing plays. So he does. He sends them to Walsingham. Walsingham gives them to an actor. An ambitious young man who happily signs his own name to Marlowe's plays.

He signs them, 'William Shakespeare'.

Possible? What do you think? Remember, history is not always simple or straightforward. In cases like this historians make up their own minds from the facts that they have. So, you can be an historical 'police officer'. In cases like this, what *you* think is as good as what another historian might think.

The theft of the Crown Jewels
Colin Wilson, Damon Wilson and Rowan Wilson

The saying 'You can't be too careful when choosing your friends' is certainly true of this story . . .

A villain who certainly deserved execution cheated the hangman because the King of England – Charles II – entirely lacked the spirit of vengefulness.

The infamous Colonel Blood was born in Sarney, County Meath, in Ireland, in 1618, and christened Thomas. His grandfather lived in Kilnaboy Castle, and was a Member of Parliament. Blood's father was a prosperous blacksmith who owned an ironworks. When the Civil War broke out in 1642, Blood hurried to England to fight on the side of King Charles I. But as it became clear that Cromwell's forces were going to win, he changed sides and joined the Roundheads. The result was that when Charles was defeated in 1653, Blood was made a Justice of the Peace and granted a large estate.

His prosperity lasted only seven years; when Charles II returned to the throne in 1660, Blood had to flee back to Ireland. He was not entirely destitute – he had married a Lancashire heiress, who had borne him a son. In Ireland he joined a plot with other disgruntled Cromwellians to seize Dublin Castle and take its governor, Lord Ormonde, prisoner; it failed and he had to flee again, this time to Holland. After taking part in more political plots, he became a marked man with a price on his head. A daring rescue of a fellow conspirator, who was being taken to London under an escort of eight soldiers, again made Blood one of the most wanted men in the kingdom. In spite of this, he returned to England in 1670, and, under the name of Ayloffe, practised as a doctor at Romford.

He still dreamed of revenge on Lord Ormonde, who had dispossessed him and crushed his Irish plot. On 28 May 1670, Ormonde was on his way to a banquet in the Guildhall when he was held up in his coach and dragged out by several men. Blood then told him that he was going to be hanged at Tyburn, and sent the others off to prepare the gallows. But the coachman raised the alarm, and servants ran to Ormonde's aid; Blood fired a shot at him, then ran into the shadows of Piccadilly. (It was rumoured that he escaped with the aid of the Duke of Buckingham, who would have been glad to see Ormonde hanged.)

Back in Romford, he decided on an even bolder scheme: stealing the Crown Jewels, which were kept in the Tower of London, behind a grating in a locked basement room.

The keeper, Blood learned, was a man named Talbot Edwards, who lived with his family on the floor above the jewels. So one day early in 1671, disguised as a parson, Blood went to see the Crown Jewels, and became friendly with Talbot Edwards. Next time he went he took his wife. But as they were leaving the basement of the Martin Tower, Mrs Blood had a sudden violent stomach ache, and was taken into the Edwards' apartments to rest. The grateful Parson Blood returned a few days later with four pairs of white gloves for Mrs Edwards.

Blood was soon a regular visitor. And since Talbot Edwards had a pretty daughter, he was delighted when Blood proposed a match with his own wealthy nephew, an idea that his womenfolk also received with enthusiasm.

On 9 May 1671, Parson Blood arrived at 7 a.m. with his 'nephew' and two more companions. While the good-looking young man was making the acquaintance of the ladies, Blood suggested that they might see the Crown

Jewels. Edwards thought it a good way of passing the time and led the way downstairs. He unlocked the door of the room that held the jewels, led them in, and locked it behind him. At that moment, he was knocked unconscious with a mallet wielded by Blood.

The thieves wrenched away the grating that protected the jewels, and removed the crown, orb and sceptre. The crown was flattened with the mallet and stuffed into a bag, the orb stuffed down the breeches of one of the men. Edwards, who had been tied up, began to struggle at this point, and Blood ran him through with his sword. The sceptre was too big to go into the bag, and one of the accomplices – Blood's brother-in-law, Hunt – began to file it through.

Then there was an interruption. Edwards' son had been serving in Flanders, and he now arrived unexpectedly. Blood's 'nephew', looking out of the window, saw him approaching and made an excuse to go downstairs. Blood decided that it was time to leave; they dropped the sceptre and hastened away.

At this moment, Edwards regained consciousness, and began to shout 'Treason! Murder!' The son, now upstairs with his mother and sisters, ran down to see what was the matter. When he found his father bleeding from a sword wound, he raised the alarm.

Blood shot a sentry who tried to stop him, then made a minor mistake that betrayed loss of nerve: instead of leaving across the nearest drawbridge, by the Bulwark Gate, he changed his mind and made for the Iron Gate, near which his horse was tied. Even so, he came close to escape – the sentries mistook other guards for the fugitives and attacked them. Fortunately, the commander of the guard recognized the mistake, and reached Blood as he was mounting his horse. Blood pointed his pistol and pulled the trigger; it misfired. Beckman wrestled with

Blood and finally overcame him. By this time the three accomplices had also been arrested.

In custody, Blood refused to answer questions, repeating stubbornly: 'I'll answer to none but the King himself.' Blood knew that the King had a reputation for liking bold scoundrels, and reckoned on his Irish charm to save his neck.

He proved correct. Blood was taken to the Palace, where he was questioned by the King, Prince Rupert, the Duke of York, and other members of the royal family. Charles was amused by his roguery, and chuckled when Blood remarked that his escapade had not been worth it, since the Crown Jewels were certainly not worth the £100,000 they were usually valued at – £6,000 would be nearer to it. Blood then went on to invent a tale of a plot to murder the King in which he himself had taken part. They had hidden, he explained, in the reeds at Battersea when the King went to the river to bathe, but 'such was the awful majesty of your unclothed form that the weapon fell out of my hand'. The King may have taken this as a flattering reference to his natural endowments; at all events, he asked, 'What if I should give you your life?' and Blood answered promptly, with the correct expression of deep humility, 'I would endeavour to deserve it, sire!'

Blood was not only pardoned – to the disgust of Lord Ormonde – but granted Irish lands worth £500 a year. With his pockmarked face, short legs and little blue eyes, he soon became a familiar figure around central London, and made frequent appearances at court.

Talbot Edwards, who recovered, was also rewarded by the King, and achieved his own kind of celebrity as the man who had been robbed of the crown by Colonel Blood. He lived to a ripe old age, always delighted to tell the story to visitors.

Blood's downfall came eight years later, when, in 1679, he quarrelled with his former patron, the scheming Duke of Buckingham. Somehow, perhaps when drunk, Blood came to accuse Buckingham of 'gross immorality'. Buckingham sued him for £10,000 – which would have ruined Blood – and, to Blood's dismay, he was found guilty. But immediately after the verdict, Blood fell ill, and died on 24 August 1680, at the age of sixty-two.

Even death was not quite the end of the story. There was soon a rumour that Blood had arranged his own 'death' to escape paying the fine, and that the coffin contained some other body. The coffin was dug up in the presence of the coroner; when the body had been identified at an inquest it was reburied – a disappointment to his enemies, who still hoped to see him hanged.

Crime doesn't pay
Nigel Blundell

Does crime pay or doesn't it? Read the following accounts to see how a number of criminals got themselves into particularly sticky situations.

Perhaps the ultimate story of the crook who realised that crime is not worthwhile is the tale of the bandit who walked into a bank in Davenport, Tasmania, put a bag on the counter and told the girl teller: 'Fill it up – I've got a gun'.

The girl started to empty the tellers' tills until the robber stopped her at $5,000 and told her: 'That's enough for me.'

Minutes later he reappeared, put the loot back on the counter and told the girl: 'Sorry, miss, I didn't really want to rob you.' Then he calmly waited for the police to arrive.

Another would-be bandit handed a bank cashier in Delray Beach, Florida, a badly-spelled note which read: 'I got a bum. I can blow you sky high.' The cashier showed it to his colleagues and they all fell about laughing. The would-be thief was so embarrassed that he ran away.

After robbing a garage in Reno, Nevada, a gunman allowed the owner to make just one phone call. He did – to the police.

Finding that his unfortunate victim had no cash, a mugger in Essex forced him to write out a cheque. 'My name is Andrew Cross – make it out to me,' he ordered.

His victim promptly went to the police, armed with the name of his assailant.

A bank robber at Portland, Oregon, handed a cashier a slip of paper which read: 'This is a hold-up and I've got a gun.' The cashier gave a nod and waited while the man scribbled another note: 'Put all your money in a paper bag,' and handed it across the counter. Turning the note over, the cashier wrote: 'I don't have a paper bag.' The man ran off.

The 75 convicts who tunnelled out of a jail at Saltillo, in northern Mexico, slipped up on the planning. After six months of hard digging for freedom, they emerged in the nearby courtroom where most of them had been sentenced to time behind bars.

Forgers are often caught by their printing mistakes. But a Kenyan crook who produced near-perfect banknotes was easily identified, thanks to his vanity. Instead of a portrait of the president, he used a picture of himself.

Three prisoners from Lincoln were hitching a lift when a bus stopped for them – and out jumped seven warders from their jail who recaptured them. The 'bus' contained a prison party on its way to court.

Nothing went right when an Italian decided to rob a bank in Milan. He tripped on a doormat as he burst in, and fell over.

His mask dropped from his face and his revolver accidentally went off. He got up, ran towards a cashier and slipped over again, grabbing the counter to get his balance.

His gun fell to the floor. With staff and customers laughing at his bungling, the humiliated thief decided to make his exit. He ran out of the door and collided with a policeman who was standing on the pavement writing out a traffic ticket for his illegally-parked getaway car.

A cool Southampton crook strolled into a city supermarket and filled a basket with goods. He gave the check-out girl a £10 note, intending to snatch the contents of the opened till. But it contained only £4.37, which he nevertheless took – losing £5.63 on his criminal shopping spree.

A hapless hold-up merchant disguised his identity by placing a pillowcase over his head and dashed into a store in Riverside, California.

After crashing into several display counters, the bandit realised that he should have cut eye-holes in the mask. He raised the pillowcase to find his way out of the store, was recognised by a customer and later arrested.

A man charged with purse-snatching in Tulsa, Oklahoma, denied the charge and opted to present his own defence. He began by asking a woman victim: 'Did you get a good look at my face when I grabbed your bag? . . . Err . . .' He was immediately found guilty and jailed.

A gunman who robbed a Paris grocery store lost his hat as he ran away. Written inside were his name and address, and police were waiting for him when he got home.

A Denver bandit crashed his getaway car into a lamp-post but escaped on foot.

Arriving home, however, he fumbled for his latch key while still holding his gun – and shot himself in the leg.

Two British burglars came across a camera in the house they were raiding and, for fun, took photographs of each other with their loot. Unfortunately for them, they dropped the camera as they made their escape, and police returned it to its owner, a 75-year-old Tyneside woman. Three months later she had the film developed, and the two raiders were swiftly identified and arrested.

A mugger on the tourist island of Majorca tried to snatch the handbags of two German great-grandmothers, both aged 77. They overpowered him, locked him in the boot of their car and drove him to a police station.

Safebreakers in England's West Midlands tried to cut through a metal door with an oxy-acetylene torch. Unfamiliar with the device, they failed to turn up the oxygen supply and consequently spent hours cutting a hole large enough to put a hand through. Only after they were captured and brought to court did they learn that the safe door had not even been locked.

A burglar stole a budgerigar in a raid on a house in Rochdale, Lancashire, because he thought his own budgerigar needed some company. But the stolen budgie, called Peter, got his own back by 'shopping' the burglar to the police. When detectives visited the raider's home, Peter was able to identify himself by giving his name – and a good impression of the owner's ringing telephone.

A burglar trying to make a getaway after setting off the alarm in a do-it-yourself store in Chesterfield, Derbyshire, was faced with a choice of twelve doors, each complete with brasswork and hinges. But they turned out to be display models, each opening onto a blank wall. After trying them all in darkness, the man climbed a staircase, only to fall back down, knocking himself out.

A man and a woman were arrested for fare dodging by transport police in New York when they tried to get a free ride. The bus they chose was carrying 75 people to court, all about to be charged with fare dodging.

Three men who stole 31 rainbow trout owned by a Mr Herring were caught by police led by Sergeant Pike.

A driver in Oklahoma City was fined for being drunk in charge of a car and of stealing a horse, which was found sitting beside him in the passenger seat at the time of the arrest.

Finally, thieves who raided a home in Tooting, London, stole two dozen sealed bags. Police never recovered the bags but they do not believe the raiders enjoyed their haul. The bags contained hundreds of thousands of fleas.

Activities

A little stabbing

1   Mrs Bull did not believe the story Frizer and his friends told her. Make a list of the things she did not believe.

2   When these men were tried in court they were found not guilty. Giving reasons, explain whether you would have agreed or disagreed with this verdict.

The theft of the Crown Jewels

3   Make a list of the major events in Colonel Blood's life.

4   An obituary is a summary of someone's life, written just after their death. They are usually honest accounts and highlight the major events in someone's life story. Imagine you are a journalist. Write the obituary that might have appeared in a newspaper for Colonel Blood. The list you made before will help you.

Crime doesn't pay

5   Imagine that you are producing a TV programme called *The Good, the Bad and the Very Stupid*. Your researcher has sent you the extract called 'Crime doesn't pay'. You have to choose six items from this to feature in your first programme. Write an e-mail to your researcher explaining which six stories you are going to use, in what order you will use them, and why those six interested you most.

Remember that in an e-mail you must type in who the document is for and the subject of the e-mail, e.g.

Name: Gareth Harvard
Subject: Literary Project Update

Overall

6   Produce a 'Wanted' poster for one of the criminals mentioned in this section.

7   Create a police file for a criminal of your own invention. Try to make sure that your character and their crime sound convincing. You should include a physical description of the person, their last known address and any other addresses with the years they lived there also noted, a list of known acquaintances and any relevant previous history.

Travel

People have always loved to travel, be they great explorers or regular holidaymakers. We can experience new and wonderful things by visiting other places. And if this is impossible, we can read about other people's travels. Maybe this is why travel writing is so popular – it gives us a chance to widen our horizons even when an actual trip cannot be managed.

This section presents a view of three different types of traveller. But even though each one is completely different, they all share a love of new places and experiences.

Iowa
Bill Bryson

Bill Bryson is a travel writer. In this extract he remembers his childhood in Iowa and the holidays spent away from it with his family.

My father liked Iowa. He lived his whole life in the state, and is even now working his way through eternity there, in Glendale Cemetery in Des Moines. But every year he became seized with a quietly maniacal urge to get out of the state and go on vacation. Every summer, without a whole lot of notice, he would load the car to groaning, hurry us into it, take off for some distant point, return to get his wallet after having driven almost to the next state, and take off again for some distant point. Every year it was the same. Every year it was awful.

The big killer was the tedium. Iowa is in the middle of the biggest plain this side of Jupiter. Climb onto a roof-top almost anywhere in the state and you are confronted with a featureless sweep of corn for as far as the eye can see. It is 1,000 miles from the sea in any direction, 400 miles from the nearest mountain, 300 miles from skyscrapers and muggers and things of interest, 200 miles from people who do not habitually stick a finger in their ear and swivel it around as a preliminary to answering any question addressed to them by a stranger. To reach anywhere of even passing interest from Des Moines by car requires a journey that in other countries would be considered epic. It means days and days of unrelenting tedium, in a baking steel capsule on a ribbon of highway.

In my memory, our vacations were always taken in a big blue Rambler station-wagon. It was a cruddy car – my dad always bought cruddy cars, until he got to the male menopause and started buying zippy red convertibles – but it had the great virtue of space. My brother, sister and I in the back were miles away from my parents up front, in effect in another room. We quickly discovered during illicit forays into the picnic hamper that if you stuck a bunch of Ohio Blue Tip matches into an apple or hard-boiled egg, so that it resembled a porcupine, and casually dropped it out the tailgate window, it was like a bomb. It would explode with a small bang and a surprisingly big flash of blue flame, causing cars following behind to veer in an amusing fashion.

My dad, miles away up front, never knew what was going on and could not understand why all day long cars would zoom up alongside him with the driver gesticulating furiously, before tearing off into the distance. 'What was that all about?' he would say to my mother in a wounded tone.

'I don't know, dear,' my mother would answer mildly. My mother only ever said two things. She said, 'I don't know, dear.' And she said, 'Can I get you a sandwich, honey?' Occasionally on our trips she would volunteer other pieces of intelligence like, 'Should that dashboard light be glowing like that, dear?' or, 'I think you hit that dog/man/blind person back there, honey,' but mostly she wisely kept quiet. This was because on vacations my father was a man obsessed. His principal obsession was with trying to economise. He always took us to the crummiest hotels and motor lodges, and to the kind of roadside eating-houses where they only washed the dishes weekly. You always knew, with a sense of doom, that at some point before finishing you were going to discover someone else's congealed egg-yolk lurking somewhere on your plate or plugged between the tines of your fork. This, of course, meant **cooties** and a long, painful death.

But even that was a relative treat. Usually we were forced to picnic by the side of the road. My father had an instinct for picking bad picnic sites – on the apron of a busy truck stop or in a little park that turned out to be in the heart of some seriously deprived ghetto, so that groups of children would come and stand silently by our table and watch us eating Hostess Cupcakes and crinkle-cut potato chips – and it always became incredibly windy the moment we stopped, so that my mother spent the whole of lunch-time chasing paper plates over an area of about an acre.

In 1957 my father invested $19.98 in a portable gas stove that took an hour to assemble before each use and was so wildly temperamental that we children were always ordered to stand well back when it was being lit.

---

cooties: body lice

This always proved unnecessary, however, because the stove would flicker to life only for a few seconds before puttering out, and my father would spend many hours turning it this way and that to keep it out of the wind, simultaneously addressing it in a low, agitated tone normally associated with the chronically insane. All the while my brother, sister and I would implore him to take us some place with air-conditioning, linen table-cloths and ice-cubes clinking in glasses of clear water. 'Dad,' we would beg, 'you're a successful man. You make a good living. Take us to a Howard Johnson's.' But he wouldn't have it. He was a child of the Depression and where capital outlays were involved he always wore the haunted look of a fugitive who had just heard bloodhounds in the distance.

Eventually, with the sun low in the sky, he would hand us hamburgers that were cold and raw and smelled of butane. We would take one bite and refuse to eat any more. So my father would lose his temper and throw everything into the car and drive us at high speed to some roadside diner where a sweaty man with a floppy hat would sling hash while grease-fires danced on his grill. And afterwards, in a silent car filled with bitterness and unquenched basic needs, we would mistakenly turn off the main highway and get lost and end up in some no-hope hamlet with a name like Draino, Indiana, or Tapwater, Missouri, and get a room in the only hotel in town, the sort of rundown place where if you wanted to watch TV it meant you had to sit in the lobby and share a cracked leatherette sofa with an old man with big sweat circles under his arms. The old man would almost certainly have only one leg and probably one other truly arresting deficiency, like no nose or a caved-in forehead, which meant that although you were sincerely intent on watching *Laramie* or *Our Miss Brooks*, you found your gaze being drawn, ineluctably and sneakily, to the amazing eaten-away body sitting beside you. You couldn't help yourself. Occasionally the man would turn out to have no tongue, in which case he would try to engage you in lively conversation. It was all most unsatisfying.

After a week or so of this kind of searing torment, we would fetch up at some blue and glinting sweep of lake or sea in a bowl of pine-clad mountains, a place full of swings and amusements and the gay shrieks of children splashing in water, and it would all almost be worth it. Dad would become funny and warm and even once or twice might take us out to the sort of restaurant where you didn't have to watch your food being cooked and where the glass of water they served you wasn't autographed with lipstick. This was living. This was heady opulence.

Where coal was king
Peter Hain

People have very different ideas about what makes a good holiday. Whilst thousands of people were lying on the beach, Peter and Pat Hain set off with two friends to tramp across the hills of Wales on foot. This is Peter's record of that walk.

After the first couple of hours I wondered whether we would ever finish our planned 85-mile summer walk through the South Wales valleys. Although my rucksack had only the essentials, my back and shoulders were killing me.

None of us had ever attempted such a venture before. Friends and family thought we were mad. But, through the six days, things actually got easier. Inner socks and comfortable boots meant the feared blisters did not arrive. The aches eased as our bodies adapted and we got fitter.

Our initial 10-mile route took us via the signposted Glamorgan Woods Way through rugged forestry tracks to stay our first night in the Pelenna International Mountain Centre perched above Tonmawr, another former mining village.

Locals report periodic sightings of the Beast of Margam, said to be a puma-like cat: it was hard not to worry about this as we pushed past miles of conifers, their undergrowth pitch black, within yards of the track. In another Neath valley, a man walked into similar forestry one day and was never found.

We arrived shattered. But a shower and a meal revived us enough to catch a lift down to the Colliers Arms in nearby Pontrhydyfen.

We had determined always to leave after an early breakfast, so as to conquer a good few miles early in the day. The dew fresh, it was down the mountain, pools of sun slanting through the firs. We passed through Afan Argoed Country Park where waymarked walks and cycleways fan out from a Countryside Centre and Welsh Mining Museum.

That evening, we arrived at the hilltop village of Llangynwyd. Never have four guests flopped down so thankfully at Mrs Jones's B&B. It was becoming a test of resolve. Twenty-two miles gone and not even a third of the way.

During the evening, we relaxed in the Old House, an ancient pub-restaurant with scenic views and huge portions of good-value food: it's so popular you can't book, and people come from miles around. It was said to be the calling place of Wil Hopkin, an odd-job man who, according to local legend, was prevented from marrying a rich landowner's daughter; the tale of the Maid of Cefn Ydfa tells how her father locked her away and she died of a broken heart.

We viewed with foreboding the next day's 18-mile stint to Llantrisant. It seemed impossible. But, by this time, our friends Dave and Pauline Wilson were captivated by the breathtaking scenery. Used to walks in neat, picturesque Devon, they hadn't imagined South Wales could be such an attraction for visitors and hikers.

The Devon coast was in sight one moment, the Mumbles next. The conifered forests of West Glamorgan had given way to rolling hills, sandstone ridges, beautiful meadows and woods, with a collage of purple heather, yellow gorse and blue bilberries. The weather continued sunny with a nice breeze.

In the distance was the Taff Ely windfarm. It took ages to get there and we flopped down to rest, the windmills towering above, dwarfing the landscape.

Then we got lost. The excellent signposting on the Ridgeway Walk degenerated. With the medieval hilltop town of Llantrisant a mile away, our footpath disappeared under brambles and merged into the new hospital site. A kind member of the construction team gave us a lift over the last mile and dropped us on cobbled streets to walk the last few yards and check in at the New Inn.

This was the only real right-of-way trouble we'd had, though, the next morning, we encountered a huge brooding white bull in a field; he was untethered, but didn't seem remotely interested as we shuffled nervously by.

We were heading for Cardiff's Castell Coch at the mouth of the Taff valley. A fairytale Victorian folly, it can be seen from the M4 to the south, brightly lit at night.

The steep descent towards the castle seemed to take ages but, to our delight, we suddenly encountered the Gwaelod-y-Garth pub and took a welcome breather.

By the end of each afternoon, all of us were obsessed by the prospect of luxuriating self-indulgently in hot baths.

In Pontypridd, hospitality was unexpectedly provided by David John, the owner of the excellent Market Tavern hotel, which offers three-star accommodation at B&B prices.

By now we were returning to the coalfield heartlands. Our route overlooked the Rhondda. Occasional coal outcrops could be spotted where, in the old days, people might forage in the winter with a pick and shovel. In today's jobless era, the hard times are back: £750 was recently spent prosecuting a valley father who stole £2-worth of coal to keep his wife and new-born baby warm.

In the middle of nowhere, Llanwonno appeared out of the forestry. This isolated spot has only a church, a graveyard – and, most important, a pub.

By late afternoon we had reached the Dare Valley Country Park outside Aberdare. Its green pasture lands have been reclaimed from coal tips. Right in the middle there's a homely farmhouse, the Greenmeadow Riding Centre. Its garden teems with animals, including Vietnamese goats and other unexpected exotics.

The next morning we awoke gung ho: just 13 miles to go. Over the mountains we entered anthracite country. An occasional lorry passed us from one of the private licensed mines. Some still use pit ponies. A few are little more than rat holes and accidents are frequent: two men have died in the past three years.

Just below our route, a workers' buyout at Tower Colliery, the last British Coal pit to close in South Wales, now has unprecedented productivity and success. The walk had taken us from the past of coal and back to the future. There are now about 1,000 miners in the valleys where once more than a quarter of a million worked.

The walk back down in triumph to Resolven reminded us how painful it had been going the other way. It was almost surreal getting home to celebrate: had we *actually* done it?

We were fortunate with the weather. But the valleys need more than sunshine and spectacular scenery to attract walkers.

All the good work done by Forestry Commission, local authority and tourist officials needs to be better co-ordinated and publicised so that the world outside realises just what wonderful walks there are in the valleys – the equal of any across Britain.

Across the Atlantic
Charles Lindbergh

If you want to travel between Europe and America today, you can book a ticket and hop on a plane. In 1927, no one had ever flown non-stop between New York and Paris. Mind you, several people had died trying to do it.

This is how Charles Lindbergh described the start of his 2950-mile solo flight starting just outside New York.

Thirty revolutions low! The engine's vibrating roar throbs back through the fuselage and drums heavily on taut fabric skin. I close the throttle and look out at tense faces beside my plane. Life and death lies mirrored in them – rigid, silent, waiting for my word.

Thirty revolutions low – a soft runway, a tail wind, and overload. I glance down at the wheels. They press deeply, tires bulging, into the wet, sandy clay.

The wind changed at daybreak, changed after the *Spirit of St Louis* was in take-off position on the west side of the field, changed after all those barrels of gasoline were filtered into the tanks, changed from *head* to *tail* – five miles an hour *tail*!

A stronger wind would force me to the other end of the runway. But this is only a breath; barely enough to lift a handkerchief held in the hand. It's blowing no faster than a man can walk. And if we move the plane, it may shift again as quickly as it did before. Taking off from *west* to *east* with a tail wind is dangerous enough – there are only telephone wires and a road at the far end of the field – but to go from *east* to *west* would mean flying right over the hangars and blocks of houses beyond – not a chance to live if anything went wrong. A missing cylinder and – 'Hit a house. Crashed. Burned.' – I can hear the pilots saying it – the end of another transatlantic flight.

And there's no time. There's no time to move the plane – so small, so delicate, so heavy – two and a half tons on those little tires, with all the fuel in. It would have to be towed, and towed slowly, five thousand feet over the muddy runway. We'd have to send for a tractor; I couldn't taxi – the engine's too light – it would overheat – the fuel tanks would need topping off again – hours lost – night would fall on the Irish coast. I'm already late – it's long past dawn – and the weather reports say *clearing*.

My cockpit quivers with the engine's tenseness. Sharp explosions from the exhaust stacks speak with confidence and precision. But the *Spirit of St Louis* isn't vibrant with power as it's always been before. I'm conscious of the great weight pressing tires into ground, of the fragility of wings, of the fullness of oversize tanks of fuel. There is in my plane this morning, more of earth and less of air than I've ever felt before.

Plane ready; engine ready; earth-inductor compass set on course. The long, narrow runway stretches out ahead. Over the telephone wires at its end lies the Atlantic Ocean; and beyond that, mythical as the rainbow's pot of gold, Europe and Paris. This is the moment I've planned for, day and night, all these months past. The decision is mine. No other man can take that responsibility. The mechanics, the engineers, the blue-uniformed police officers standing there behind the wing, everyone has done his part. Now, it's up to me.

Their eyes are intently on mine. They've seen planes crash before. They know what a wrong decision means. If I shake my head, there'll be no complaint, no criticism; I'll be welcomed back into their midst, back to earth and life; for we are separated by something more than the few yards that lie between us. It seems almost the difference between the future and the past, to be decided by a movement of my head. A shake, and we'll be laughing and joking together, laying new plans, plodding over the wet grass toward hot coffee and a warm breakfast – all men of the earth. A nod, and we'll be separated – perhaps forever.

Thirty revolutions low! 'It's the weather,' the mechanic said when I climbed into the cockpit. 'They never rev up on a day like this.' But his encouraging words failed to hide the apprehension in his voice and eyes. Now, the expression on his face, out there behind my silver wing, shows more clearly than any words what is passing through his mind. He's gone over the engine piece by piece, helped tear it down and put it back together. He feels sure that every part is perfect, and firmly in place. He's squirmed into the tail of the fuselage to inspect structure and controls. He knows that wheel bearings are freshly oiled; that air pressure is up; that tires are rubbed with grease to keep the mud from sticking. He's double-checked the thousand preliminary details to a flight. His work is done, done with faithfulness and skill. Now, he stands there helplessly, intent, with tightened jaw, waiting for my signal. He feels responsible for the engine, for the plane, for me, even for the weather that holds the revolutions low.

I lean against the side of the cockpit and look ahead, through the idling blades of the propeller, over the runway's wet and glistening surface. I study the telephone wires at its end, the shallow pools of water through which my wheels must pass, and the top-heavy black column of smoke, rising from some source outside the field, leaning indifferently in the direction of my flight. A curtain of mist shuts off all trace of the horizon.

Wind, weather, power, load – how many times have I balanced these elements in my mind, barnstorming from some farmer's cow pasture in the Middle West! In barnstorming a pilot learns to judge a field so accurately that he can tell from the size of his passenger, and a tuft of grass tossed to the wind, just where his wheels will leave the ground, just how many feet will separate them from the boundary fence and trees beyond. But here, it's different. There are no well-established standards from which to judge. No plane ever took off so heavily loaded; and my propeller is set for cruising, not for take-off. Of course our test flights at San Diego indicate that it *will* take off – theoretically at least. But since we didn't dare try a full load from Camp Kearney's stony ground, the wings now have to lift a thousand pounds more than they ever carried before – five thousand pounds to be lifted by nothing more tangible than air.

Those carefully laid performance curves of ours have no place for mist, or a tail wind, or a soft runway. And what of the thirty revolutions lost, and the effect of moisture on the skin? No, I can turn to no formula, the limits of logic are passed. Now, the intangible elements of flight – experience, instinct, intuition – must make the final judgement, place their weight upon the scales. In the last analysis, when the margin is close, when all the known factors have been considered, after equations have produced their final lifeless numbers, one measures a field with an eye, and checks the answer beyond the conscious mind.

If the *Spirit of St Louis* gathers speed too slowly; if the wheels hug the ground too tightly; if the controls feel too loose and **logy**, I can pull back the throttle and stop – that is, I can stop if I don't wait too long. If I wait too long – a few seconds will decide – well, another transatlantic plane

---

logy: dull or heavy

crashed and burned at the end of this same runway. Only a few yards away, two of Fonck's crew met their death in flames.

And there's the added difficulty of holding the wheels on the runway while sitting in a cockpit from which I can't see straight ahead. A degree or two change in heading could easily cause a crash. The runway is narrow enough under the best of conditions; now – with the mud – and the tail wind – and the engine not turning up –

I lean back in the wicker seat, running my eyes once more over the instruments. Nothing wrong there. They all tell the proper story. Even the tachometer needle is in place, with the engine idling. Engine revolutions are like sheep. You can't notice that a few are missing until the entire flock is counted. A faint trace of gasoline mixes with the smell of newly dried **dope** – probably a few drops spilled out when the tanks were filled. I turn again to the problem of take-off. It will be slow at best. Can the engine stand such a long ground run at wide-open throttle, or will it overheat and start to miss?

Suppose I *can* hold the runway, suppose I *do* get off the ground – will fog close in and force me back? Suppose the ceiling drops to zero – I can't fly blind with this overload of fuel; but the wheels have doubtful safety factors for a landing. Shall I cut the switch and wait another day for confirmation of good weather? But if I leave now, I'll have a head start on both the Fokker and the Bellanca. Once in the air, I can nurse my engine all the way to Paris – there'll be no need to push it in a race. And the moon's past full – it will be three weeks to the next one; conditions then may be still worse.

Wind, weather, power, load – gradually these elements stop churning in my mind. It's less a decision of logic than

---

dope: protective varnish used on the fabric parts of an aircraft of feeling, the kind of feeling that comes when you gauge the distance to be jumped between two stones across a brook. Something within you disengages itself from your body and travels ahead with your vision to make the test. You can feel it try the jump as you stand looking. Then uncertainty gives way to the conviction that it can or can't be done. Sitting in the cockpit, in seconds, minutes long, the conviction surges through me that the wheels *will* leave the ground, that the wings *will* rise above the wires, that it *is* time to start the flight.

I buckle my safety belt, pull goggles down over my eyes, turn to the men at the blocks, and nod. Frozen figures leap to action. A yank on the ropes – the wheels are free. I brace myself against the left side of the cockpit, sight along the edge of the runway, and ease the throttle wide open. Now, in seconds, we'll have the answer. Action brings confidence and relief.

But, except for noise and vibration, what little effect the throttle has! The plane creeps heavily forward. Several men are pushing on wing struts to help it start – pushing so hard I'm afraid the struts will buckle. How can I possibly gain flying speed? Why did I ever think that air could carry such a weight? Why have I placed such reliance on a sheet of paper's curves? What possible connection is there between the intersection of a pencil's lines in San Diego and the ability of *this* airplane, *here*, *now*, to fly?

The *Spirit of St Louis* feels more like an overloaded truck than an airplane. The tires rut through mud as though they really were on truck wheels. Even the breath of wind is pressing me down. A take-off seems hopeless; but I may as well go on for another hundred feet before giving up. Now that I've started, it's better to make a real attempt. Besides – it's just possible –

Gradually the speed increases. Maybe the runway's not too soft. Is it long enough? The engine's snarl sounds inadequate and weak, carrying its own note of mechanical frustration. There's none of the spring forward that always before preceded the take-off into air – no lightness of wing, no excess power. The stick wobbles loosely from side to side, and slipstream puts hardly any pressure against rudder. Nothing about my plane has the magic quality of flight. But men begin stumbling off from the wing struts. We're going faster.

A hundred yards of runway passes. The last man drops off the struts. The stick's wobbling changes to lurching motion as **ailerons** protest unevenness of surface. How long can the landing gear stand such strain? Five thousand pounds crushing down upon it! I keep my eyes fixed on the runway's edge. I *must* hold the plane straight. One wheel off and the *Spirit of St Louis* would ground-loop and splinter in the mud. Controls begin to tighten against the pressure of my hand and feet. There's a living quiver in the stick. I have to push hard to hold it forward. Slight movement of the rudder keeps the nose on course. Good signs, but more than a thousand feet have passed. Is there still time, still space?

Pace quickens – turf becomes a blur – the tail skid lifts off ground. I feel the load shifting from wheels to wings. But the runway's slipping by quickly. The halfway mark is just ahead, and I have nothing like flying speed – The engine's turning faster – smoothing out – the propeller's taking better hold – I can tell by the sound. What r.p.m.? But I can't look at instruments – I must hold the runway, not take my eyes from its edge for an instant. An inch off on stick or rudder, and my flight will end.

The halfway mark streaks past – seconds now to decide – close the throttle, or will I get off? The wrong decision

---

aileron: a movable, hinged section mounted near the trailing edge of an aeroplane wing and used to control balance

means a crash – probably in flames – I pull the stick back
firmly, and – *The wheels leave the ground*. Then I'll
get off! The wheels touch down again. I ease the stick
forward – almost flying speed, and nearly 2000 feet of
field ahead – A shallow pool on the runway – water spews
up from the tires – A wing drops – lifts as I shove aileron
against it – the entire plane trembles from the shock – Off
again – right wing low – pull it up – Ease back on to the
runway – left rudder – hold to centre – must keep straight
– Another pool – water drumming on the fabric – the next
hop's longer – I could probably stay in air; but I let the
wheels touch once more – lightly, a last bow to earth, a
gesture of humility before it – Best to have plenty of
control with such a load, and control requires speed.

The *Spirit of St Louis* takes herself off the next time –
full flying speed – the controls taut, alive, straining – and
still a thousand feet to the web of telephone wires. Now,
I *have* to make it – there's no alternative. It'll be close, but
the margin has shifted to my side. I keep the nose down,
climbing slowly, each second gaining speed. If the engine
can hold out for one more minute – five feet – twenty –
forty – wires flash by underneath – *twenty feet to spare!*

Green grass and bunkers below – a golf links – people
looking up. A low, tree-covered hill ahead – I shallow-
bank right to avoid it, still grasping the stick tightly as
though to drop a wing for a turn, hardly daring to push
the rudder. The *Spirit of St Louis* seems balanced on a pin
point, as though the slightest movement of controls
would cause it to topple over and fall. Five thousand
pounds suspended from those little wings – 5000 pounds
balanced on a blast of air.

The ground's farther underneath; the plane's climbing
faster – I'm above the trees on the hilltop! Plenty of
height, plenty of power – a reserve of it! Two hundred
feet above the ground. Now, if the motor starts missing,

there are places I might land – level fields between the hills and highways. The landing gear would give way, and the fuel tanks would burst; but if I cut the switch, at least there's a chance that the fuselage would skid along and not catch fire.

Now I'm high enough to steal glances at the instrument board. The tachometer needle shows 1825 r.p.m. – no sign of engine overheating. I move the throttle back slowly – a glance at the terrain ahead – a glance at the tachometer in my cockpit – 1800 – 1775 r.p.m. Pull the stabiliser back a notch. The air speed's still over 100 miles an hour – I throttle down to 1750 – the tail stays up – the controls are taut! Then the curves are right. If the *Spirit of St Louis* can cruise at 1750 r.p.m. with this load, I have *more* than enough fuel to reach Paris.

And yes, he did make it to France. It took him thirty-four hours to make the journey and the most dangerous part turned out to be landing amongst the enormous crowds at the airport outside Paris!

Activities

Iowa

1 Write down what you learn about Iowa.

2 Imagine that Bill Bryson is being interviewed for a holiday programme. He is asked to give advice about the things you should and should not do on a family holiday. What questions is the interviewer likely to ask him, having first read this extract? What advice do you think Bill Bryson is likely to give in his replies?

Where coal was king

3 Imagine that you are writing a leaflet for the Welsh Tourist Board about this walk. Include the route details – sights to look out for and places to stay. Remember that you are trying to encourage tourism and that your comments should therefore be positive.

4 Now write an advertisement for a walk, event or place for the tourist board in your area. Include details of three photographs you would include and say why you have chosen them.

Across the Atlantic

5 Make a list of the preparations made before take-off and described here. Make a list of the emotions that Lindbergh felt before and during take-off.

6 Imagine that you are a radio news reporter present at the take-off. Describe to your listening audience how the mechanic prepared the plane for the journey, and then the take-off itself. Remember to make it sound exciting, and try to get across how Lindbergh was likely to be feeling at the time and the dangers he faced.

Radio broadcasters have to paint a picture in words for the listening audience. Check your work to make sure that it gives your audience a clear idea of what is happening.

Overall

7 Write about a journey or holiday that you have been on. You might write about a particularly good holiday or journey you had, or about a holiday or journey where everything went horribly or amusingly wrong.

1939–1945

When the bombs fell and the tanks rolled during the Second World War, the effects on people's lives were strikingly different. For some people it even brought advantages such as time off school! For others, it resulted in tragedies that they would remember for the rest of their lives. Here are three accounts of how young people were affected by that war.

Bombs and beachcombing
Dorothy Thomas

Dorothy Thomas lived in a town on the south coast of Wales and was thirteen when the War broke out. One of her first thoughts was whether they would get a longer holiday. Here is her account of what actually happened.

We were issued with gas-masks and identity cards, and an Anderson shelter for the garden. At school we had our air-raid drill. It was a real anticlimax. Rationing, and what was going on overseas, didn't mean much to me. People were called up, and every street had a team of men who practised dealing with incendiary bombs. Nothing much happened for some time. There was the occasional air raid, but I got used to getting up at night and going to sit in the shelter.

The war really began for us with the 'Three Nights' Blitz' of Swansea in February 1941. The sirens sounded at 7.45 p.m. on the first night. First came the flares which lit up the town like daylight. We felt very vulnerable, sure we could be seen cowering in our shelter. Then came the incendiaries, like Christmas lights. Then the bombs. They continued for hours.

I never listened to Lord Haw-Haw's broadcasts from Germany, but news got around that he'd promised another raid for Swansea on the following night. I felt uneasy. When the siren sounded again at 7.45 p.m. exactly I began to panic. It was just like the night before. The following night Lord Haw-Haw announced that they would be back again – he even forecast which districts would receive special attention. I lived in one of them. It was the worst of the three nights. In the early light of morning I saw houses that had collapsed like packs of cards. Some had their roofs intact, but lying on the ground. People I knew lay buried beneath. I saw half an Anderson shelter balanced on top of a chimney. Where were the occupants? I grew up quickly during those three nights.

Everyone who had anywhere to go left Swansea the next day, including my mother, my brother and myself. My father was in the police so he stayed behind. We walked to High Street station through the ruins of a prosperous town. Craters lined the road full of smoke, water or unexploded bombs, with a little notice advising pedestrians not to fall in the hole. Our train stayed until no more people could squeeze aboard then pulled away from what was left of Swansea.

A month or so later we moved to a remote house on the Gower peninsula, just a stone's throw from the sea. My father would visit us on his day off. We shared our house with a lady who had lived in Canada and told me about the Red Indians who looked at her through slits in her log cabin. The house was haunted. We fetched our water from a stream and we had no electricity or telephone. Our only lavatory was at the end of a kind of garden maze, much frequented by adders. It was a two-seater earth closet, and if the wind was blowing the wrong way the toilet-paper you put in one hole blew up and flew away out of the other. As we had no newspapers and only a battery radio, the war seemed very distant. Even the postman found it too far to walk down the sheep track to our door, so we collected our mail in the village.

I spent most of my time on the beach seeing what the tide brought in. Sometimes I found emergency rations from a plane or ship. What luck! Plenty of chocolates and raisins. Once a mangled bit of an aeroplane was washed up on the shore. I seized hold of it, and found a little mouse nestling on board. I caught him in some wet sand and put him in a box. However, he had gone by morning, so perhaps he was a German mouse determined to escape.

I was often worried by the threat of invasion. Our long beach was such a suitable place for an enemy landing. Once the army came and stuck lines of stakes like pit-props in the sand. They were to prevent boats coming ashore, but they were washed away after a few days. A pill-box was built on the dunes as well, but I never saw any soldiers defending it. I used it as a shelter when it rained. If we were invaded the church bell was to be rung, but we lived so far from the church we didn't think we'd hear it. A friend promised to let us know if the bell rang. Early one morning it did. There was a rope from the vicarage to the belfry so the vicar could toll the bell without having to run across his churchyard. After a stormy night the rope had slackened and it lassoed an unlucky farmworker on his way to the morning milking. The more he struggled to free himself the louder the bell rang. We heard it all right, but our friend never came to tell us it was a false alarm.

Aeroplanes practised shooting on part of the beach. One trailed a target for others to attack. We weren't supposed to be there: the entrance to the dunes was closed off with barbed wire, and behind the wire were mines. I went there just the same. I must have been crazy. I was ready to run like hell if the shooting began.

Mines often floated in with the tide. The coastguard shot them and they exploded with a terrific bang. One evening I watched a mine come in that seemed to be heading straight for our house. I told the coastguard, but he said it wouldn't go off unless it hit a pebble. The next morning my mother, very anxious, looked for it out of the bedroom window, and as she couldn't see the mine she assumed it had been washed out to sea. I went to the beach and saw the mine close inshore, hidden from the house by a bank of sand. I went round it on tip-toe. The points were pearly pink. Later the bomb disposal men came and blew it up.

An enemy was washed up once. There was much discussion as to whether he should be buried in the churchyard. Most people were against. His body was carted away and I never discovered what happened.

In the spring I had to collect gull's eggs. I didn't like it. The gulls didn't either, and swooped down at me. The eggs were large. They weren't very nice boiled or fried, but were good for cakes if a bit fishy. They were a useful addition to our rations along with the salmon bass my father used to catch.

I ran wild for about six months and then I was sent to a commercial school in Swansea. When I came home on winter nights the walk along the side of the hill was long, and very dark. I only had a small torch because of the black-out. Every morning I left my wellington boots in a farm shed. When I put them on in the evening to go home the evacuees from the farm had often dropped half a dozen little potatoes into each boot.

In about 1944 the ghost that haunted the house made my mother decide to return to Swansea. She preferred to take her chance with the hazards of war than with the supernatural.

I still walk on the same beach whenever I can. The track from the beach to the house can hardly be seen any more. My mother, my father and my brother are all dead. My love of the sea, particularly just here, and our old home, is as strong as ever. Had it not been for the war perhaps my life would have been in some ways the poorer.

Alarms
John Gordon

John Gordon's memories of the first part of the War are quite different. If he hoped to miss school, he was unlikely to mention it: his father was a teacher! In fact his first concern at the start of the War was not bombs or guns, but babies. He explains it like this:

I was fifteen and babies horrified me. The smell of talcum powder or of washing drying indoors had always plunged me into misery – another new baby to turn the house upside down and punish me for the sin of just being there. But there hadn't been a baby for years and I thought all that was finished with . . . and then, one day I saw a carton of food for 'expectant mothers' half hidden on the larder shelf and I realized that my mother was pregnant.

Nobody had mentioned it and I had managed not to see her increasing size, but now the bulge in her pinafore, which I had tried to ignore, was just what I had feared. I kept the guilty knowledge to myself.

This was no way to welcome a brother. I woke up one morning and was told that my mother, taken to a nursing home in the night, had given birth to a baby boy. I pretended it was news but I could not pretend to be happy – unlike another morning soon afterwards when I shouted downstairs to ask what the score was. My father called up, 'A hundred and eighty-five for the loss of three of ours.' The Battle of Britain and my brother Frank came almost together.

The numbers of planes shot down in the battle were as much a fantasy as Shakespeare's tally of the dead at

Agincourt, but I believed them. They helped me to ignore Frank, until one day I saw him very frightened.

We all carried gas masks in little square boxes slung from our shoulders – millions of cardboard boxes had been got ready for the purpose before the war and, although we didn't know it, there were also stockpiles of cardboard coffins – but there were no tiny gas masks for babies. If a gas attack came, babies were to lie in rubber bags with a big window and be supplied with air filtered through a concertina pump at the side. We had one, but only one attempt was ever made to get Frank buttoned up inside it. He was so terrified that no one ever tried again, and the baby 'mask' lay under the stairs for the rest of the war.

But seeing a helpless baby pushing out its bottom lip in real terror worked on me, as it always had in spite of the competition I felt from babies. I could never bear to see the younger ones take risks; any sort of threat to them turned me into a mother hen in an instant (which was something else I had against them), so I would make them cling tight on every fairground ride and would worry if they took on dares. And, as it happened, Frank grew up more like me in almost every respect than the others.

I was jealous of them, yet had to protect them. Not that Norman, two years younger than me, ever needed my protection from anything. He was an extrovert and popular, everybody's idea of what a mischievous little devil should be, unlike me with a load of cares on my shoulders; and David was good-looking and gentle, dark and different to the rest of us, and girls melted for him. Elizabeth, the girl my mother had always wanted, had plenty of admirers and led a girl's life which was foreign to us lads. The Gordons, however, were a clan and we clung together, even though very often I didn't want any part of it.

We were too crowded to have evacuees but my father was not going to be left out of the war. He became an officer in the Army Cadet Force at his school and he was an Air Raid Warden. On top of this he took on evening classes to help keep his family and clerked for a fruit firm in the holidays. When he was at home he was asleep in his chair.

He smoked heavily, rolling his own cigarettes with pipe tobacco, and this and the overwork brought on the TB which, at the end of the war, made him lose a lung and almost killed him.

Sometimes he would take me with him to spend a night at the Air Raid Wardens' post, where we slept fully clothed on camp beds until the sirens sounded. Then there would be telephone calls to report to other posts or we would patrol the streets to make sure no lights showed. The bombers were not interested in Wisbech but we heard the throb of the German planes, quite different to the steady drone of the British and American, as they filed by in the darkness to their targets in the Midlands.

One quiet night, when no siren had sounded and we were lying on our beds, I heard the thump of explosions and woke my father. We rang around but nobody had anything to report and I felt foolish. At dawn, however, we went out exploring and found a string of craters across a field on the outskirts of town. No houses had been damaged so nobody had thought it worthwhile to tell us, but the bombs had been pretty big judging by the size of the holes. I slid down into one and it was a perfectly smooth hemisphere with a little dome of hard, compacted earth at the very centre. I found a fragment of bomb case down there.

Not all bombs were so wide of the mark. One overcast day when we were all at home except Dad there was a howl in the sky like a diving Spitfire. We were running out to see it when the howl rose to a shriek, the air contracted and expanded in a gigantic clap of thunder, there was a split second of silence and then a rain of bricks and fragments that punched holes in slates and clattered into gardens.

I tried to make my mother take shelter under the stairs – a bit late by then, after the bombs had fallen – but the German bomber, a Junkers, circled again with its machine gun knocking like a hammer in the sky.

I went to fetch Dad from his workshop at school. 'We thought we heard a plane,' he said. 'Did it drop anything?'

'I'll say it did!' and my indignation made him and the teacher with him burst out laughing.

The bombs had come down just beyond the end of our road, aimed at the gasworks, but they missed the target and the whole stick had fallen along a row of little houses beside a railway track. We went to look. One side of the street was jagged heaps of bricks, with rooms suddenly exposed and furniture hanging from upper rooms over piles of rubble. Men clambered over it in the drizzle.

My father helped to search for survivors but only one person was killed, a woman. A man who had been on night shift and was asleep in bed had been blown across the street, still in his bed, and landed unhurt on the roof of a house opposite.

Alongside the railway line lay the leg of a dog. It was there for weeks.

Who will be next?
Walter Buchignani

Régine Miller's experience of the War was affected almost from the beginning by the German occupation of Belgium. Nor was this the only problem, because her family was also Jewish. The first couple of years of the War had their problems, but the crunch came in 1942.

That summer, the terrible summer of 1942, the more the Allied bombers flew over Belgium, the worse the German orders against the Jewish people.

The deportations had started in March. Unmarried men between the ages of sixteen and forty were singled out for the labor camps. They were to be put to work erecting German fortifications along the northern coast of occupied France.

Léon was sixteen years old.

The knock came early one morning. Her father answered it. Her mother was resting in bed. At first it didn't seem too serious. The person at the door was a young man. He said he'd been sent to deliver a message to Léon Miller.

The young man was around Léon's age. He seemed nervous standing in her father's shadow. Léon leaned over and whispered in Régine's ear. 'I know that guy. He went to my school.'

'Is he your friend?' Régine asked.

'No, but I know him.'

The young man handed the envelope to her father and turned to leave.

'Hold on,' her father said. 'What's this about?' He opened the envelope, took out the paper and unfolded it.

Régine saw the look of anger spread over her father's face. The young man, more nervous now, turned to go. Her father crumpled the paper and let it drop to the floor. He shoved the young man, and Régine heard him yell out as he tumbled down the stairs. Her father picked up the crumpled ball of paper and threw it down after him.

'What's going on?' her mother called in a weak voice from the bedroom. 'Is something wrong?'

Her father slammed the front door and marched into the bedroom. She heard him say that Léon had to report to the train station in the morning. 'We'll ignore the notice,' he said.

'How can we ignore it?' her mother asked.

Her father did not answer.

A little while later there was another knock on the door. The same young man handed Mr. Miller another notice and ran quickly back down the stairs. Régine's father closed the door slowly, reading the new notice.

Her father again walked into the bedroom, followed by Léon. Through the open door Régine saw her father and brother sit down on the edge of the bed. Her father explained the notice to her mother. 'Léon must go to the train station,' he said, his voice a whisper.

There was no choice in the matter. If Léon didn't go, the whole family would be taken away.

A few days later Régine was sent away to a summer camp run by Solidarité. She should have enjoyed it, but thoughts of her brother came back, not just at night before she went to sleep, but even in the daytime when she tried to laugh with the others.

When Régine came home from camp a month later, her mother was back in the hospital.

Régine remembered the first time her mother entered the hospital. It was the only time she ever saw her father cry. Régine had visited her every afternoon after school with her father and brother, and the three of them stayed until the nurses told them to leave.

Régine had sat on the edge of her mother's bed and told her everything she was learning in school. Mademoiselle Descotte, her teacher, had shown the class how to knit, and Régine promised to teach her mother when she came back home.

Régine kept her promise. She showed her mother how to knit. Léon, too, wanted to learn, and the three of them knitted a long scarf. But her mother had changed. She had even less energy. She took the medicine from the bottles that bore a skull and crossbones on their labels and every few months she returned to the hospital for injections that left her covered with bruises.

Now back from camp and again standing at her bedside in the hospital, Régine was shocked to see how much thinner her mother had become. The hand held out to her seemed only bones, not at all like the strong hands that had ground nuts and stretched dough over the tabletop. Her mother tried to smile at Régine but the pain came through in her mother's voice as she spoke: 'I'm sorry you have to see me like this.'

Her father stood by in silence and remained silent during the walk home. That evening Régine found out why.

Her father sat Régine down on the sofa in the flat and sat down beside her. 'I have something important to tell you,' he began. He looked more nervous than she had ever seen him. 'You know Monsieur Gaspar, don't you?'

Monsieur Gaspar was the father of Jeanne Demers, the upstairs neighbor whose husband had been taken away by the Germans. She had moved out but her father had stayed on. He and Régine's father always stopped to talk when they met on the stair landing.

'I was speaking with him just this morning,' her father said. 'He said maybe we should get some help.'

'Yes?'

'He said we should find someone who will take care of you. Just for a little while. I think it's a good idea.'

Régine frowned. 'You mean Madame Sadowski?' Régine Sadowski was a family friend. But the last time she had helped while Mrs. Miller was in the hospital, she mixed the separate dishes kept for meat and dairy. Régine's mother had been very upset when she came home.

'No, no,' her father said. 'Monsieur Gaspar told me about someone else. Another woman. You will stay at her house.'

'At her house?'

'Yes. Just for a little while.'

'Who is she?' Régine asked.

'She's very old,' said her father. 'Her name is Madame André, and she lives alone in Boitsfort.'

Boitsfort was a suburb of Brussels, and Régine thought it must be far because you had to take more than one tram to get there.

'Must I go, Papa?' she asked.

'Yes,' her father said. 'It's best this way.'

'What about you?' Régine asked.

'I have work to do here. Your mother is safe in the hospital. And you will be safe in Boitsfort. All the arrangements are made.' It was clear from his tone of voice that he did not want to explain any further. 'I'll take you there in the morning.'

This was unbearable. First her brother had been taken away, then her mother was taken to the hospital, and now to be separated from her father. He must have seen the look in her eyes.

'It will only be for a little while. She will take good care of you. And you can keep her company. She's very old. Monsieur Gaspar told me she's seventy-eight.'

'Will you visit?' Régine asked.

'Every week,' he said. 'I promise.'

They went into the bedroom to pack. Her father worked quickly. He pulled a duffel bag out of a closet and picked among her clothes. As he threw them on the bed, Régine noticed that none of the clothes he chose bore the yellow Star of David.

'Don't I have to wear the star?' she asked.

'No,' her father said, angrily.

Régine understood now why her father was sending her away, why he wanted her to go live with a stranger. It had nothing to do with her mother's illness. That was just an excuse.

The Germans had taken Léon away. Did her father fear she might be next? It had to do with what had happened at La Gare du Midi.

Régine remained 'hidden' by various families for three years. Her mother, her father and her brother Léon all perished, probably in the gas chambers of the Auschwitz concentration camp. After the War, Régine went to live with an uncle in England. She married a survivor of the concentration camps and had two children, Sonia and Philip. In 1958 they moved to Canada, where she still lives.

Activities

Bombs and beachcombing

1   List the changes that the War brought to Dorothy
    Thomas's life. Then make a 'top ten' chart of the ones
    you think were most important.

2   If you had been Dorothy Thomas's brother or sister, what
    would you have enjoyed, and what would you have
    hated, about what was happening?

Alarms

3   Make a list of facts about the Gordon family.

4   Make a spider diagram showing how John Gordon felt
    about the things going on around him. It might start
    like this

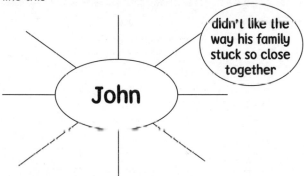

didn't like the
way his family
stuck so close
together

John

5   Try writing entries for the sort of diary you think John
    Gordon might have kept at the time.

Who will be next?

6   You have the opportunity to interview Régine about the
    summer of 1942. What would you ask and how might
    she reply?

Overall

7 Imagine two of the young people in this section were able to meet and talk about the War. What would they say?

8 'The War was not as bad for children as people sometimes suggest.'

Prepare a speech to support or argue against this statement in a debate. Base it on evidence in this section and any further information you are able to collect.

Advice

Many newspapers and magazines have advice sections where readers can write in and ask for help. You have probably seen these yourself. In this section, the writers talk about the types of things that concern all of us as we grow up – from how to cope with parents' evenings to surviving your first crush (or, in the case of 'Crashing the pain barrier', simply surviving).

Crushes
Anita Naik

What is a crush? Have you ever experienced one – for a stranger glimpsed on the bus, a pop star, the boy or girl next door? Can crushes damage your health or seriously improve it? Read on to discover the answers.

The symptoms of a crush are familiar enough: a drifting in thought and behaviour, a feeling that no one else in life has ever felt this way, and a conviction that this person you love is your ideal mate. Falling into a crush nearly always happens in the same way. You see someone you like and fancy. It could be a boy down the street, a movie star, a pop star, a teacher. You may have seen them before and never given them a second look, but suddenly you begin to feel that this person could be the man for you. Then you start to imagine what this person is like, where they go, what they feel strongly about, etc. At this stage, most people turn into super-detectives in their pursuit of information.

Long before I knew anything about Tom Cruise, I knew he was a lovely man. He's always nice in all his roles and has a really kind face. I didn't really know much about him to begin with so I started buying any magazine with articles about him in it. I've got quite a collection now and I can tell you anything you want to know about him. Who his agent is, what his mother's name is and what he was like at school. I also know where he lives and his likes and dislikes. Reading interviews with him just backs up all the things I've imagined to be true about him.

Julia (16)

After the initial collection of information, you then start to think about them more and more, using the information you have gleaned. This is when a crush really moves onto a more serious footing, because this is the moment when you start believing that you really know this person. You also become convinced if you had the chance to meet him, he'd fall for you and you'd go out.

Gavin is a boy who works in my local record shop. He's also in a local band and I always fancied him because we had a lot in common. Once the local paper did a piece on him and I cut it out and put it on my wall because it backed up everything I already thought about him. I spend hours imagining what it would be like to kiss him, to go out with him, what our children would look like and how when he notices me he'd realize how much he loves me. I can't help loving him because he is everything I want from a boyfriend and none of the guys round here match up to that.

Sally (17)

Of course, lots of people have crushes just for the sake of them, and why not? They can be fun and very enjoyable. You don't need to have a specific reason for having a crush, and you don't have to do anything when you've got one. Lots of girls jump from one crush to another, replacing one man with another, just for the fun of it.

I'm the first to admit I have a different crush every week. Last week it was David, a guy I work with on Saturdays; today it's an actor I saw in a film last night. I don't think there's anything wrong with it because I'm not actually hurting anyone. I'm 16 years old and I don't want to tie myself down to a particular boy, so it's far more fun to have crushes and far less trouble.

Anna (16)

Despite the popular notion that girls with crushes are giggly, silly, and out of their minds, most girls aren't like this. Knowing a crush isn't real is part of the fascination. It's all pure escapism, designed to give pleasure not despair.

Of course, I know my crush isn't real. I'm never going to meet this man, he's an actor and he lives in Hollywood. If I do ever get there, he'll be married and well out of reach. I do this all for fun. It's exciting to imagine another life in my head. It cheers me up when

I'm miserable, and is fun to talk about. Some people get so annoyed when they hear me talk about him. They seem to think I'm being silly and I should pull myself together. But why should I? These are my own fantasies. I don't tell them what to think so I don't see why they feel they can tell me!

Sue (17)

The positive side of crushes can inspire quite life-changing results, but, likewise, the negative side can produce equally devastating effects. Many girls feel guilty about having a crush. They feel that there's something not quite right about the idea of having one, and, hence, something not quite right about themselves. They worry that having a crush means they are weak willed, pathetic, and useless.

I don't tell too many people about my crush because I know what their reaction will be. They either laugh or tell me to get a life! I know they think I'm stupid and secretly bitch about me behind my back.

Lorna (15)

Like anything, crushes aren't always exciting and fun; like love, they come with a frustrating and miserable side. They have the power to make you feel depressed, anxious, and downright fed up.

The worst thing about Rob is that I know I'm the right girl for him. The trouble is he doesn't see me enough to realize this. To him I'll always be the little girl who lives next door. It's all so upsetting, we get on so well, but he never gives me a chance. He's going to live in America for a year and I know he's going to fall in love with someone there and then I'll have lost him for ever because of circumstance and nothing else. Whenever I think of this I get so depressed.

Zoe (16)

The fact is, crushes are to do with feelings, and this means they come tied up with adverse as well as positive effects. Any thing or person who has the ability to reach down inside you and touch a part that no one else can, brings distress as well as happiness. For some, the distress comes from the realization that nothing concrete can ever happen, while for others the frustration of being so far but so near is too hard to handle.

I dream of Paul every day, I imagine us going out and doing all the normal things couples do. The truth is he is married and doesn't know I exist. But I know if only he had met me before he met his wife, things would have been so different. When I think of this I get so depressed because it makes my whole life feel hopeless.

Mandy (17)

Living in Never-Never Land is dangerous and depressing. It's no good hoping against all hope that one day you'll just meet your crush, and, lo and behold, he'll fall madly and passionately in love with you. The chances of this happening are minute; no one is saying you and your crush can't make a go of it, but love at first sight is a highly overrated notion. Love takes time to grow, and no amount of wishing can make it appear on the spot. Being madly in love with a pop star/actor/boy across the road is fine, but when you start to believe you're cheated out of a relationship with that person the effects can be devastating. Life suddenly becomes frustrating and unbearable because every moment is spent wishing you were with the man you love at the expense of your everyday life.

The parents' evening
Rosie Rushton

The book from which the next extract comes is designed to prepare people for the change from primary to secondary or high school. This section deals with that awful moment when the parents actually get to meet the teachers.

After you have been at school a couple of terms, a new joy will be thrust upon you and your family, the Parents' Evening. In some schools, the parents will be invited to chat with the staff while you sit at home watching telly and worrying about what they are saying behind your back. In more progressive 'Let's all be one big happy family' schools, you will be asked to go along as well. It is debatable whether it is better to be there, where you can keep an eye on what is going on and put your oar in when necessary, or to be at home where you don't have to hear what they are saying about you.

WHEN YOU ARE INCLUDED

Taking parents anywhere is a risk: letting them loose in a room full of teachers is fraught with danger. For one thing, they are all on the same side – the 'getting the best out of the boy/girl' team. You need to know what you are letting yourself in for.

TAKING YOUR TURN

You will get a note informing your parents that they have five minutes with each member of staff in order to

facilitate the maximum flow of bodies. It sounds like a
very good idea but it never works. There you are, with the
freshly combed Father, queuing patiently to see the Head
of French while the parents of Cecilia Descartes are
holding forth at great length about their child's
Mediterranean background, her penchant for languages
and her sensitive nature. Poor Mr K makes weak and
ineffectual attempts to draw the conversation to a close.
You and your parents have three courses of action:

1 Move to another queue. No good; the same thing will
   repeat itself, only this time it will be Mr Vocal thumping
   his fist on the table and demanding to know why
   Jeremy is not in the top set for English.

2 Pretend that you are about to faint, in the hope that
   Mother Descartes will remove her buttocks from
   the chair and let you collapse into it and make a
   rapid recovery.

3 Go home. (Not good, this – it labels your family
   as uninterested and that is a very rude word in
   the staffroom.)

Whatever you do, try to prevent the by now weary
parent from complaining out loud. Remarks such as 'If I
ran my business like they run a Parents' Evening, we
would all be bankrupt' are unlikely to endear your family
to the Head.

Once you get to see the teacher in question, there are
more hazards to be overcome.

1 Getting found out. Remember all those little white lies
   you told your father? Like the C that you pushed up to
   a B minus? Or the Maths test that you said you got 7 out

of 10 for because 4 didn't sound very good? Well, I can promise you that Mrs Higgins will take great delight in producing said piece of work from her little black folder and offering it to the parents to read. You will notice a tightening of the paternal lip and a heightening of the maternal cheek colour. This means trouble when you get home. The only remedy is to come clean in future. It saves an awful lot of hassle later.

2 Handling the conversation. Different teachers have different approaches to Parents' Evening. Some will gush and grovel to your parents in such a sickening manner that you have a keen desire to throw up; others will try to impress with their aloof superiority; and yet others will seem totally bored.

WHEN YOU ARE LEFT AT HOME
While at first sight, sitting at home watching *The New Baywatch* seems infinitely preferable to sitting at school hearing about your failed Geography exam, it is not without its problems.

1 By the time your parents get home, they are tired, have sore bottoms from sitting on school chairs with sagging seats and are gasping for a coffee. If they have heard good reports of you, they will pat you on the back, tell you to keep it up and let you go to bed. If they are worried about your algebra, batting averages and grasp of European History, they will want to talk. Be patient with them.

2 Parents do worry. It is a fact of life, like autumn following summer and tights only laddering where it shows. If they nag a bit about your work, don't stamp your feet/

scream/throw the *TV Times* at them. If it's bad because you don't understand, say so. If it's bad because the subject holds no interest, tell them. And if you know it's just because you've been a bit lazy, confess. They'll be far more understanding than you imagine.

3 Say 'Thanks for going.' No, I am not going loopy – some parents just don't bother to go, which makes their kids feel a bit left out. You might not like the speech on neat handwriting and learning to spell that follows, but at least they show they care.

While I doubt there are more than a handful of kids and parents who can put their hands on their hearts and swear that they love Parents' Evenings (except the mummy and daddy of William the Whizz Kid who gets straight A's and never misses the goal-post), they are there to be endured. And remember, your parents will be dreading them as much as you. After all, whose genes is it that determine your brain power?

THEY DO HAVE A POINT

Before you bite your parents' heads off or write your teacher off as a nag, remember, they do have a point. They've been there, done it and got the T-shirt. And what's more, believe it or not, they know what you can do and are there to make sure you do it.

Crashing the pain barrier

Aidan Macfarlane and Ann McPherson

Very few people are fortunate enough to get through life without having an accident of some kind. Some young people are unluckier than others, as this extract shows . . .

Wednesday 30th January

Have had a major accident and am stuck indoors, so may as well start writing my diary again. Last Saturday started OK. Sam called and we went off on our bikes to visit a friend of ours called Joanna, as Sam had a record she wanted to tape. They disappeared upstairs leaving me feeling a right wally. Then Nick, another friend of ours, arrived and took my bike, so for a laugh I rode Sam's round the close. As I am fairly short in the leg I couldn't really handle it, and going down the steep hill I suddenly couldn't find the brakes. At the bottom was a row of houses and a sharp left turn. Still searching for the brakes, I slid on some ice and hit the kerb. As I flew over the handlebars I heard something going CRACK – a sound I'd heard before not long ago – and that was it.

Next thing I remember was being in the ambulance. The driver and his mate were laughing and telling jokes. I couldn't understand what had happened. My jeans were ripped, my left arm was blown up in a plastic bag so I couldn't move it, and my head hurt like hell. Everything was coming and going, and I felt sick and faint. There was no siren blaring. The driver's mate said they only used that in real emergencies, or when they wanted a cup of tea in a hurry!

When we finally stopped and they opened the back doors there were Mum, crying, and Dad, white-faced. Dad started swearing and telling me what a bloody stupid thing it was to do, and had I done it on purpose to worry them, and why didn't I think about these things before I did them? Honestly, grown-ups! Mum told him to shut up. I wanted to get out of the ambulance by myself, just to show I was all right, but the ambulance men pushed me back, wrapped me in a red blanket like I was eighty or something, and carried me out in a sort of chair. They said I'd broken my arm and the blown-up plastic bag was to keep it still and stop it hurting. Mum clutched my good hand and Dad dragged along behind, muttering about Sam being furious over the scratches on his bike.

They wheeled me into a little white room and put me on a hard bed. Nobody seemed to bother much about me, though I could hear someone saying something outside about a tetanus injection. Mum had to go out and ask if I could have something for my pain – and came back saying that the nurse was sorry but they were busy. At last a nurse came and shoved a thermometer in my mouth and held my wrist. If she wasn't as pretty as the nurses on telly she was certainly as nice. She helped me take my torn jeans off. My poor legs looked all white and were covered in grazes. My heart nearly stopped when I thought she was going to take off my underpants too.

A man came in and asked me questions about the accident, and some silly things like what day was it and who was the Prime Minister? He looked into my eyes with a light, stuck pins into my legs to see if I could feel, hit my ankles, and then examined EVERY last bit of me. Finally felt brave enough to ask what it was all about. He said it was to make sure I hadn't done any damage to my brain – like being concussed. Turns out that this is like bruising your brain, but it gets all right in the end. The 'silly questions' were to make sure it was functioning OK.

Nobody seemed to have actually DONE anything yet, then a lady came in and started examining me again. Wondered just how far SHE was going to go. She explained that the man was a medical student and learning, and that she was the actual doctor and was going to arrange for my head to be X-rayed to make sure none of my skull bones were broken, and my arm because she was sure that it was broken. More waiting and nothing being done. Began to want to be home in my own bed.

The lady doctor showed me the X-rays and said I was lucky not to have dented my skull and damaged my brain. She said she couldn't understand why people didn't wear crash helmets when cycling, because 300 cyclists are killed and 30,000 injured each year. If I was thinking of getting a motorcycle in the future, I would HAVE to wear one. But even so, 1,000 motorcyclists are killed on the roads each year, and 63,000 injured. To emphasize the point, she said that she spent most of every day putting together people who had had accidents, and that in any one year:

One in every 11 motorscooter riders
Onc in every 16 motorcycle riders
One in every 56 car drivers

are killed or involved in an accident. It doesn't even seem safe to walk around, as 1,900 pedestrians are killed and 60,000 injured each year. All this doesn't even include other types of accidents like drowning which kills over 100 children a year, or the 2 million people treated by the hospital for home accidents each year. HELP!

Asked the doctor if she wore a crash helmet when she bicycled. She went pink and didn't answer. Mum gave me one of her special looks and said I seemed to be getting better. Dad went back to work and Mum stayed while they put sloppy wet white bandages on my arm which made it warm. Bit by bit the bandages grew hard and smooth and I was left with a lovely shiny white plaster for my friends to write on. This stops the ends of my broken bones moving so that they can heal properly.

Just as I thought everyone was finished there was one more thing – an anti-tetanus injection. The dirt in the cuts on my knee might have contained tetanus bacteria. This could give me lockjaw, which is spasm of the muscles of your body, not just your jaw, and can easily kill you. Mum said I had last had the injection when I was five but that it only protects you against tetanus for about ten years and then you need it again.

Because I'd been knocked out, they said I might have to stay in the hospital for the night. This frightened me at first, but then I thought it might be quite fun, especially if all my friends came to see me with presents. However, I was allowed home with my mum because everything seemed all right, but with instructions that she should bring me back if I began to throw up, had a bad headache, saw double, or became drowsy because of the knock on my head. They also said to come back if the fingers of my broken arm became numb, swelled up, or became white or blue. Sounded nasty but didn't happen. The last four days have been boring, which is why I am writing all this.

Nobody's been to see me except Sam – to complain about his bike. Though he did manage to ask me how I felt. Then he went on about how some girl called Jane in our class was soft on him. Dad said that I've suffered enough and that he'd pay for the repairs to Sam's bike. He can be great sometimes. Susie and Sally have been sympathetic too. If I haven't many friends, I suppose having sisters is better than nothing.

Thursday 31st January

Up early to catch the bus – first day back in school. Was the centre of attention for five seconds while everyone defaced my plaster with graffiti, some of which I feel embarrassed to be carrying around in public. Had to sit out and work during the sports periods. Don't usually like sport but, now I can't do it, feel left out. Mr Jones, the sports teacher who helps run the school magazine, said that as I had nothing better to do I'd better be the form representative for the magazine and get some articles for the next edition. Told my mates about my accident (with a few embellishments about my bravery and my attractiveness to the nurses) but found I could hardly get a word in. Turned out everyone thought they'd had a worse accident than me and were going to tell me about it whatever happened. Got fed up and told them to write about their troubles for the school magazine.

Thursday 7th February

A whole week without writing. Too exhausted by my one-handed efforts at home and in school. All the teachers have stopped making allowances for the fact that I'm a cripple. Stories for magazine coming in well. The things my form mates seem to get up to . . .

I broke my nose right across the bridge. I was standing with my brother and he was shaking the rain off his hair and I walked into him and broke my nose. It gave me headaches, and a purple and very embarrassing nose. I went to the hospital and first they said I would have to wait till the swelling went down. Then they sent me to the ENT clinic. No one was really sympathetic about it.

About three years ago I was hoovering in the hallway. A piece of paper would not go up the hoover so I pushed it in with a knife, and my fingers got sucked in and all cut up. Also, when I was about ten, I was sitting on the sink in the bathroom and it fell off the wall and I hit my eye and it was all bleeding.

My last injury was just over a month ago when I went ice skating for the first time. I can roller skate but I had been told by my friends that it was harder because you slip over everywhere. I went skating with some of my friends but when I got on to the ice I was very frightened because when I tried to move I slipped over. Then everything was going great until a boy behind me pushed me over and I went crashing into the side of the rink. As I did this I put my hand on the floor. Some boy who was standing next to me skated over my fingers. I started crying because I was in a great deal of pain. My friends saw me and helped me off the rink. My fingers were pouring with blood and all the skin was ripped back and my nail was cracked and bruised. After the accident I decided never to go skating again – but I did.

When I was ten I put my hand through a window. A chunk of skin came out and I was rushed to hospital. I was told I had to have a skin graft. I didn't know what that was then, and now I wish I hadn't had it because I'm still scarred and I think that I will be scarred for life. It is very embarrassing because the skin was taken from the smooth surface of my arm, and you can still see it.

Activities

Crushes

1 What are the symptoms of having a crush?

2 Why does the writer say people turn into 'super-detectives'?

3 What types of information do these super-detectives look for?

4 List the ways this writer says crushes can help people.

5 Do you think that crushes are harmless or dangerous? Write to a teenage magazine explaining your point of view.

The parents' evening

6 There is a lot of information contained in this passage. Pick out the most important information that you think Year 7 pupils need to know about parents' evenings. Use the information and your own experience to produce an A4 poster for Year 7 pupils telling them about parents' evenings. Make sure that the poster is easy to read and that it contains all the relevant information.

7 Write your own article for a school magazine giving your advice to pupils starting Year 7 in your school. You could call it 'Surviving the first term'.

Crashing the pain barrier

8 Imagine you are the mother of the boy in the story. Next day you visit a friend and tell her about your son's accident. Write out the conversation which you and your friend might have.

9 The boy in this extract is writing a magazine. His friends have told him about their own accidents and a little bit about how they happened. Choose one of the incidents and write your own imaginative story around it.

Overall

10 Now it is your turn to be the expert and give some advice. You have been chosen to give a two-minute talk to parents about one of the following:

- Why young people avoid homework and how parents can help

- How to make breakfast-time bearable

- What most embarrasses young people about their parents and what to do about it.

Write down what you plan to say in note form.

Alan Gibbons Chicken
Graham Greene The Third Man and The Fallen Idol; Brighton Rock
Thomas Hardy The Withered Arm and Other Wessex Tales
L P Hartley The Go-Between
Ernest Hemmingway The Old Man and the Sea; A Farewell to Arms
Nigel Hinton Getting Free; Buddy; Buddy's Song
Anne Holm I Am David
Janni Howker Badger on the Barge; Isaac Campion; Martin Farrell
Jennifer Johnston Shadows on Our Skin
Toeckey Jones Go Well, Stay Well
Geraldine Kaye Comfort Herself; A Breath of Fresh Air
Clive King Me and My Million
Dick King-Smith The Sheep-Pig
Daniel Keyes Flowers for Algernon
Elizabeth Laird Red Sky in the Morning; Kiss the Dust
D H Lawrence The Fox and The Virgin and the Gypsy;
Selected Tales
Harper Lee To Kill a Mockingbird
Ursula Le Guin A Wizard of Earthsea
Julius Lester Basketball Game
C Day Lewis The Otterbury Incident
David Line Run for Your Life
Joan Lingard Across the Barricades; Into Exile; The Clearance;
The File on Fraulein Berg
Robin Lister The Odyssey
Penelope Lively The Ghost of Thomas Kempe
Jack London The Call of the Wild; White Fang
Bernard Mac Laverty Cal; The Best of Bernard Mac Laverty
Margaret Mahy The Haunting
Jan Mark Do You Read Me? (Eight Short Stories)
James Vance Marshall Walkabout
W Somerset Maugham The Kite and Other Stories
Ian McEwan The Daydreamer; A Child in Time
Pat Moon The Spying Game
Michael Morpurgo Waiting for Anya; My Friend Walter;
The War of Jenkins' Ear
Bill Naughton The Goalkeeper's Revenge
New Windmill A Charles Dickens Selection
New Windmill Book of Classic Short Stories
New Windmill Book of Nineteenth Century Short Stories

How many have you read?